HOW TO COMM

2 BOOKS IN 1:

COMMUNICATION IN RELATIONSHIPS

+

EFFECTIVE COMMUNICATION SKILLS

For:

Family; Workplace.

Techniques: Persuasion; Nonviolent;

Conflict Resolution; Influence People

By

Michael Cooper

TABLE OF CONTENTS

COMMUNICATION IN RELATIONSHIPS

[SECOND EDITION]

****

A SIMPLE AND EFFECTIVE STRATEGIC GUIDE, TO IMPROVE DIALOGUE SKILLS AND MAKE COMMUNICATION CLEAR

BY

MICHAEL COOPER

INTRODUCTION

When a couple decides to enter into a more serious relationship, they want to be able to communicate at the level that they know their relationship deserves, for themselves and each other. Being able to do this effectively takes a little work and a desire to want to make sure that you are able to make sure that the bond you share with your partner grows, matures and stays strong while the two of you nurture your emotional bond as well. The ability to communicate doesn't just affect the way you talk to each other it affects your emotional response to each other as well as your intimacy with each other. Couples have an emotional intimacy that also needs to be nurtured, and it helps to make sure that you are able to keep yourselves unified as one.

When you communicate in a loving way with your partner it lets them know that you love your partner enough to want to make sure that your relationship is strong and that you can speak to each other freely and without judgment or cruelty. In a loving and healthy relationship, this is vital to make your relationship last. Communication is one of the biggest problems that people say they have is that their partner will not communicate with them and that they don't know how to fix it. Understanding healthy alternatives to non-communication is key then to understanding how to fix this problem with your partner.

To have a healthy and long-lasting relationship with your partner, there are a few things that you should learn how to do. The first being that you should learn how to become a better listener. That alone isn't enough, however. You should learn how to become what is known as an emphatic listener. This is a bit different than just regular listening. It's a special form of listening that can help strengthen your relationship because it provides you with the ability to be able to understand not only how your partner is feeling but it takes you toward the point of being able to put your partner and yourself into the mindset of caring about one another more than yourself.

Learning how to speak properly to your partner is an important tool that you will need to learn as well and the art of compromising and understanding that not everything can be your way although you can certainly get your partner to see your side. Understanding compromise in a relationship is another important aspect because many mistake compromise for letting their partner constantly have their way and thinking that this means that they can't disagree. That they constantly have to have their opinion not matter, which isn't the case at all.

When you're compromising in your relationship and in your relationship that doesn't mean you have to give the other person their way all the time and it doesn't mean that your opinion doesn't matter anymore. It simply means that your understanding where your partner is coming from and you're trying to understand how they feel while working it out together. In a relationship compromising means working together, and it does not mean that a single person gets their way all the time. Sometimes you have to let the other person have their way and sometimes they have to let you have your way. But never while compromising who you are. Understanding this is going to help your communication skills and better build your relationship.

You'll also need to understand why being yourself is so important we can't have a healthy relationship if we're not ourselves and to understand how to have a better relationship and better communication in the relationship, you'll have to know yourself and to know who you are inside and who you are in your relationship. As stated above, we should never compromise who we are and who we are inside. Knowing these things is going to help you be able to practice a more mindful relationship as well as building that intimacy that you want to develop. This book is designed to help you not only understand how to communicate with your partner better but how to enable your relationship to become more unified as well. By practicing on a day to day basis to have a mindful relationship, you will be able to achieve this for yourself and for your partner.

Being mindful in a relationship means that you're fully interacting with your partner and you're giving it your all. What you're trying to make sure of is that you are practicing behavior that leans toward that thinking of us. You think of the two of you as a couple instead of you as a partner and he as a partner. You are making your thought process more in relation to how you are with your partner. It is also the ability to be in the present moment but also has a sense of what's going on around you with yourself and your partner. This may sound complicated, but once you understand this, it's much easier than you think.

When we begin to practice the habits of a mindful relationship, it takes work because our thought process is not where it needs to be yet. Even in a relationship that has lasted over twenty years can still have the issue of one partner not being mindful of the other. As such, we need to teach ourselves how to do this so that we can have a better relationship and a more lasting love with ourselves and with our partner. We also need to make sure that we practice it as well. There's no point in learning how to be mindful of your partner if you're not willing to do anything with it. Once we began to be able to practice mindfulness every day, it becomes easier and sooner than you think you won't even have to think about practicing mindfulness because you'll do it automatically on your own. As such, your relationship will improve, and if you face these issues again, you will be able to understand how to fix them at once where you weren't able to before.

EDITOR'S NOTES

Healthy communication is a key part of any relationship. As a partner, you need to be able to communicate effectively with your significant other. Communication is so important because it doesn't just help the two of you talk to each other; it helps you learn how to strengthen the bond that the two of you have together as a couple. Everyone has heard the expression 'when you get in a relationship; two become one.' When this happens, the two of you are forming a bond of unity that is being nurtured by the love and the strength that you two have for each other and your relationship, when this bond has issues, though because of a lack of good communication, a relationship can suffer, which isn't what you want.

In any relationship, you can notice that you have issues communicating for one reason or another. This happens in any relationship at one point or another in time, and with this book, you can learn how to communicate better with your partner. It can be hard to understand exactly why you're having trouble communicating and learning how to fix it can be trickier still. In fact, many couples have this issue for years before they are able to learn how to fix this but once they do they notice that they have a better relationship and are open to speaking better with their loved one. This book offers helpful tips and reasoning for being able to utilize healthy strategies for better communication with your partner, which while strengthening your relationship as a couple. The bond between a couple is strong and beautiful, but it can be fragile at the same time, which is something that couples can work on together.

Having healthy communication strategies can help you grow as a couple and develop a better relationship because your emotional bond will grow stronger, which in turn helps your emotional intimacy as a couple. Emotional intimacy is a large part of a relationship especially in a relationship, and when you are able to strengthen this bond, you are ensuring that your partner understands that you care about them and that you are putting the time into your relationship that it deserves. Showing your partner the love they deserve and learning communication skills like empathetic listening and learning how to use empathy in your words and speech will help you be able to take your relationship to a deeper level and make sure that it can last the test of time. Every relationship needs the care of each person and understanding that in order to last, you need to be able to practice healthy communication and learn what it takes to make your relationship last. You're entering a bond of forever when you say the words 'I do,' and you need to make sure that your relationship doesn't fall into the usual traps that others fall into every day. With this book, you'll avoid this pitfall and understand that a healthy relationship is going to take a little work but is well worth the energy extended to do so.

CHAPTER 1: WHY YOU SHOULD BECOME AN EMPATHETIC LISTENER

Empathetic listening is important in a relationship and in life. When you think of empathetic listening, you may just assume it means that you think carefully, but that's not all that it is and that is actually not all there is to it. When we listen empathetically what we are actually doing is showing our partner that we care about the motives behind what they're doing or thinking. We are also showing them that we care about the situation that they're in or they are dealing with and that we want to help because we care about their feelings. The reason that this is so important in a relationship is that if you cannot communicate effectively with your partner, they're going to feel underappreciated and taken for granted. You don't want this in a relationship because that's usually one of the reasons why a relationship fails in the first place. As such, you should understand that empathetic listening is taking your ability to listen effectively and communicate to the next level.

Showing your partner that you care about where they're coming from, and you want to understand how they feel. Everyone needs to feel loved and that the person that they have chosen to spend the rest of their life with understands them and truly knows them. Your partner needs to feel like they can reach out to you if they need you. If your partner isn't able to feel that you love them and respect them, then they won't open up to you. Furthermore, if they feel like they can't reach out to you when they need you, eventually they will stop trying because they won't see the point. Instead of letting that happen, you should focus on making sure that they don't feel that way in the first place.

Empathetic listen tells your partner that you're not just spouting off the first thing that pops into your head. You're thinking before you speak and making sure that you are really considering their feelings before you speak. This is another thing that people should really remember when you're trying to be a better listener. You need to listen carefully and think before you talk. When we say things without thinking about it first, you will find that you say things that you never meant to say. This causes tension, and it causes your partner to wonder if you really meant what you have just told him. You may not have meant to say what you said, but your partner won't know that for sure unless they really know you and who you are. The ability to listen emphatically is the ability to let your partner know that you really care and that you love them.

One of the reasons that listening in this way is so important is that people need to feel felt. The two of you could have different feelings on a subject or different ideas on how something should be, but from a very basic and primary level, we want to make sure that in a conversation or in our relationship that we feel that our partner understands our point of view as well as their own. This is most especially true if we are under duress or dealing with emotions that are distressing. When we feel that we have this with our partner, it lets us feel safe and understood instead of feeling uncared for and misunderstood. One thing that you should never want is to make your partner feel as though you don't love them. This can cause unbearable harm to your relationship. As such one of the main goals that you should have is, of course, to make sure that your partner always feels that you love and appreciate them.

An important thing to remember, however, is that while listening emphatically is important this doesn't automatically mean that you have to agree with everything they say. Doing this basically shows your partner that you're not really listening to what they have to say, and instead, you're just trying to make the conversation move quickly. If you do genuinely agree with everything, they say then you need to let them know that the agreement is genuine and that you're not just patronizing or condescending to them. You need to let them know that you're not trying to shut them out or shut them down and that you genuinely agree. If you don't genuinely agree you're allowed to say so. You don't have to lie to your partner just so you can be a better listener. This doesn't help him as your partner or you as his partner.

Empathetic listening comes with many benefits that will help your relationship better and more unified. The first being that you're trying to get away from being selfish. Humans are inherently selfish by nature. Most don't want to change, but others realize that they don't need to stay that way. Although most humans are selfish learning to listen, emphatically teaches you how to move from being selfish to being selfless. This is because you're actually taking the time to do something to better your relationship and to better your relationship with your partner. Listening emphatically helps the bond between your partner and yourself as partner and partner, and it can help bring the both of you from a selfish place to a humble place where you're both thinking of each other and not just yourselves.

This is going to forge a stronger emotional connection because the two of you are leaning toward the thinking of 'we' instead of 'me.' You think of your partner instead of just yourself. This not only helps your relationship, but it helps you as a person because you're allowing yourself to grow and become more attuned to your partner and how they feel as well as yourself. This allows you to understand your partner on a much deeper level, but it allows you to know yourself on a deeper level. Listening in this way will also provide you a much more emotional bond with your partner as well as helping to build your emotional intimacy together as well. The reason for this being is that you will be able to communicate better, so your emotional response is obviously developing deeper.

Many people also have trouble understanding clarification and understanding what their partners are talking about. There have been many studies that show that men 'hear' differently than women or that women can 'hear' differently than men. This has been a popular theory since as early as 60 years ago or more, and there have been many authors that have put their own unique spin on this theory. In addition to this, there have also been just as many people wondering how to understand women and on the flip side wonder how to understand men. Most people are in the way of thinking that either is impossible to understand, but they're not. Learning how to listen emphatically helps you understand and clarify what your partner is talking about so that you can avoid these misunderstandings and help you so that you don't have to worry about not being able to understand your partner or your partner. Instead, you'll be able to converse freely with your partner, and you can avoid an argument because you'll be able to grasp what they're saying.

Another benefit from learning to listen to this way is that you will learn how to listen in a respectful manner. In addition to this, it lets you have the ability to listen to your partner and give them the undivided attention that they deserve when they're talking to you. Respect is a very big thing in any relationship and if you're not devoting your time and attention to your partner that's not going to do anything except hurt them. This happens because they will feel as if you're not taking them seriously or you don't care about what they are saying or feeling. When they're talking to you, you need to be paying attention to them as well as being able to make sure that you're giving them the undivided attention that they deserve. In a relationship, you need to make sure that you are also willing to give them your time. Another reason that relationships can fail is that one or both of you may feel neglected.

In any relationship, you also need to be nonjudgmental. Your partner wouldn't like feeling judged, and neither do you. If you know that you don't want to feel judged, why would you do it to your partner? Learning to listen emphatically gives you the ability to understand that you shouldn't be judging anyone and that they shouldn't be judging you. If you are a judgmental person, you can still change. You don't have to stay in that judgmental headspace. It is entirely possible that you can change how your mind thinks, and you can change how your attitude is toward other people and especially toward your partner. When you begin to listen in a nonjudgmental fashion, you become easier to talk to because they know that they can trust you without having to feel like they're being judged for something that they shouldn't be judged for in the first place.

A great example of this would be if your partner liked a certain sport and you didn't. You could judge them for liking that sport then you could treat them differently. This might seem like an extreme example or even a silly one, but it has been shown that sports of all things can cause an agreement. One partner likes baseball the other likes football, or one partner likes UCLA while the other likes USC. They begin to judge each other and snap at each other without actually taking the time to listen to each other and to give each other the respect that they deserve. Then they began to argue more and more, and in the end, they have a bigger problem than the one they originally started out with. A trivial issue can become much more simply because of your judging. You can like different things in a relationship, and you can have different hobbies, but that doesn't mean you have to be judged for it. Your partner shouldn't judge you, and in return, you should love them enough to do the same. Listening with empathetic ears and an empathetic heart will help you achieve this.

Another example of why empathetic listening is important is because arguments start with couples when they feel like they're not being heard, and they feel like they're being judged. In any relationship attentiveness is something that should be a part of any relationship and when you're attentive to your partner and treating them the way they deserve to be treated they tend to listen to you more as a result. Empathetic listening is going to help here because instead of going to a place of anger and a place of hostility, you'll be able to pull yourself back. This is helpful to the understanding that your partner isn't doing this on purpose and they're just not listening to you the way that they should. It is important for them to listen to you, and it's entirely possible for you to help them achieve the ability to do this better.

Practicing empathetic listening is also important because when you speak to your partner as we've mentioned before, respect is very important, so you need to be able to understand how to speak to your partner respectfully instead of being rude or hurtful. Many couples have issues talking to each other simply because they don't know how to be respectful. It can be because they weren't taught how to be respectful or they just don't speak to people how they should be spoken to but speaking to someone respectfully is a very important part of listening emphatically. If listening emphatically to your partner means that you understand where they are coming from and treating them the way they should be treated respect naturally would fall under this category. When people are rude to you, and they don't listen to what you have to say most can immediately go on the defensive and start to snap back at the people speaking to them because they feel like they've done it to them first. This can happen in a relationship as well because the couple doesn't know how to be respectful when they speak to each other. Thinking about it from this respect emphatic listening isn't just about listening respectfully it's about speaking respectfully as well.

It is also about speaking to your partner in a loving manner. Every partner deserves to be spoken to in a loving manner. There is no need to raise our voices, and there is no need to yell, scream, shout, or to belittle our partner. Instead, we should speak to our partner lovingly so that they always know that we appreciate them and that we care about them. The one thing that you should avoid when trying to communicate and letting your partner know you care is letting them know you love them. Couples had said that one reason that their relationship failed was that they did not feel that their partner loved them, and when they spoke to them, they couldn't hear the love in their voice. If you speak to your partner in a loving manner, you can avoid this problem, and you can avoid the problem of not being able to communicate lovingly together. This not only helps your relationship, but it helps keep your bond of unity strong as well.

Each and every relationship also needs one more thing. To feel and to be unified. When you get in a relationship, there is a special bond that is built between the two of you. It's precious, and though it may be strong, it can also be fragile and needs to be strengthened more and more so that the two of you as partner and partner may keep the bond between the two of you growing strong. Practicing your ability to listen emphatically will ensure that the bond between you two stays strong the way it needs to, but it also makes sure that the two of you both feel that bond inside you and you feel like you both are united together as one.

Think about listening like this. If you were in one place and your partner was in another, and you had an ocean in between what would you do? You could create a bridge, right? Then you two would be able to get to each other. Listening in this way is the same thing. When something separates you, whether it is a disagreement or agreement, you could build a bridge by using these listening skills and make sure that your partner feels that you care. By building these bridges in your relationship, you're helping yourself as well as your partner. When your down you like calling a friend or someone to talk to right? Your partner does too. Instead of a friend, though, they want to talk to you. More than that, however, they want to be heard. You can listen to someone and not hear them and the emotions that they are trying to convey.

When we talk to people, it's very easy to forget the conversation later on or even at the moment if we're not fully invested in the conversation itself. This is bad for you and your relationship for many reasons, but there are two main reasons to think about. The first being is, why are you not investing your full energy to your partner? The second being would you want your partner to do that to you.

When you're listening to your partner make sure that you're focusing as much as you can so that you will be able to remember this later, chances are your partner is going to bring this up again, and if they do, they will be sad and hurt that you didn't remember the conversation. They may think you didn't care enough to pay attention. Avoid this issue by making sure that you are invested. This helps your relationship because your partner will be able to see that you love them enough to take them seriously. In return, when they do this for you, you get to see the same care and love from them. This is important in any relationship, as both of you need to feel loved and heard.

CHAPTER 2: WHY YOU SHOULD UNDERSTAND EMPATHETIC DIALOGUE

Learning how to listen emphatically is important but being able to speak empathetically and have an empathetic dialogue with your partner is important as well, and it's the next step that you're going to need to be able to take. Empathy is a big part of how we express ourselves to each other, and it should have a place in your relationship. As said in the previous chapter, when you listen in this manner, you're able to understand how your partner is feeling and how to understand their side of the conversation. Speaking in this way is a great thing for many reasons, but there are two main ones, and they are the following. One, you speak with kindness which lets your partner feel cared for and appreciated. Two, it is about respectful speaking, which lets your partner know that you care enough to speak to them like an adult and treat them the way that they deserve to be treated. You should never speak to your partner condescendingly or like someone who is beneath you. They are not.

If you are already having trouble communicating and feel as if your already at the point of continuous arguing or issues don't pull away from your partner. Put yourself back in and understand that the first thing you need to do is to begin to fix the problems that you're having with communication. One of the first steps that you can take for yourself and your partner is to think about what you want. When we get angry or frustrated, we tend to blame our partners and get very critical. We bring up things that are bothering us, and we get very upset.

However, when we are able to realize that this is not good behavior and that it hurts our partners instead of loving them or speaking with them the way they should be spoken to, one of the best things that we can do to fix this isn't to focus on what we don't want and focus instead on what we do want and use statements that are with the word 'I'. An example of this would be the following.

Let's say that we have a couple that has been in a relationship for four years. They have no children, and the partner is in the military. Military life is very hard on many people, and it takes a very strong bond and an even stronger couple to be able to make sure that you can handle that kind of life. For this example, the partner, we will call him Kyle has come home, and the partner who we shall call Anna is upset because she feels that the partner hasn't been spending enough time with her. The wrong way to handle this situation would be the following.

Kyle comes home and sees that Anna is upset and asks what's wrong. Anna's anger explodes, and she begins yelling and making statements like 'You are never here for me,' 'You leave me here alone all day, and I have to deal with everything myself,' 'You don't care about me, and you should stay here with me.' Notice the pattern in these statements. They all have statements that use the word 'you' and are very angry and self-centered. Obviously, Anna is upset. However, this isn't going to be the way to fix this. Making statements like this to Kyle is only going to make him feel attacked, and he's going to get defensive, and one of two things will happen because of this. He will either shut down or attack back with defensiveness because he feels attacked by you. This isn't what you want or need.

The right way to handle this is if Anna made sure that she was calm and spoke in an even tone without losing her temper. If she is keeping her partner's feelings in mind as well as her own, then she will have a much better chance of getting through to her partner and helping him to understand. Instead of being accusing, she should make statements like, 'Kyle, I feel like our careers are keeping us apart more than we are together. Can we talk about how we can reconnect with each other'? Do you see the difference? She is calmly telling her partner what she needs without accusing him of being uncaring or unloving. Instead of putting him on the defensive, he will be more open and receptive to talking to her and helping her. Another example of the right way to speak is if Anna said, 'I feel overwhelmed when I feel as if I am handling everything myself. It would make me feel a lot better if I could speak to you about the problems that I am having'. This one is telling him that she is feeling so overwhelmed that she's having trouble dealing with everything on her own and that she wants to talk it out as a couple. However, this could still irritate Kyle as he could feel she doesn't appreciate the hard work that he does for the military. As such, an added statement that acknowledges him as well would help him feel that she understands his struggle as well.

Another thing that you can do is answer each other's other questions in a different way than they have before. Don't stick with a yes answer or a no answer. This is only helping to shut your partner off, which doesn't help. For example, if Anna was asking Kyle to take off of work, he could respond in the following. 'I can't take off of work because I work for the military, but what do you think we could do to help the situation?' In this way, he is acknowledging that he understands her pain and frustration, but he's also telling her that her solution is not going to work for them as a couple simply because of the job he has which is something that as a military partner she would already know. However, because he didn't flat out say no, this is letting Anna know that he is trying. As such, she could try to be more understanding in turn after seeing her partner do that as well.

You should also show your partner that you are grateful for them listening to you and trying to make the situation better. This shows that you appreciate them and their effort. Anna could tell Kyle that she appreciates that he listened to her and that she is grateful that Kyle is trying to find a solution for them as a couple to try and work through this together as a couple. Couples need to remember that relationship is a two-way street and that they have to be there for each other. Kyle listened and showed Anna that he appreciates and loves her for who she is, and she should do the same for Kyle. When disconnected couples begin to repair their relationship and begin to communicate better, your partner begins to feel appreciated and loved once again. They begin to get back into sync with each other, and they can make sure that their relationship is being healed.

If you know your personality of this is going to help, you are able to communicate better with your partner because you will understand what they need. If you're introverted for example or if your partner is introverted and you are extroverted, then obviously you're going to have some difficulty communicating simply because you're on opposite sides of the coin. Recognizing that introverts might be drained by socializing and need some recovery time would obviously affect how the two of you talk to each other. Another thing that you can do is remember to treat your partner the way that you would want to be treated and understand that if you wouldn't want your partner to talk a certain way to you, then you shouldn't talk a certain way to your partner.

This is what empathetic dialog is all about. It's about respecting your partner in the way they deserve to be respected and treated. Things are going to get tough even in the best relationships and over time communication can break down simply because you are not paying attention to each other anymore or you've stopped being able to talk to each other in the way that you need to. This is where appreciating and loving your partner naturally is going to come in. If you can accept your partner for who they are you should be able to communicate more effectively because you have no fear of judgment and you have nothing holding you back from saying exactly what you need to say. The best way to speak emphatically is to find out what is working and what isn't working. You have been practicing speaking respectively and kindly to your partner by showing compassion and empathy; now you need to put it in action. If you know that you find that the two of you are talking about the past too much or other issues that can cause issues in your relationship and the way you speak to each other than you need to have a conversation about what you're feeling and listening to your loved one and have your loved one do the same.

Remember that speaking with empathy means that you have compassion for your partner and that you are really tuned into the conversation. Show them that you understand what it is that they're feeling and what it is that they're talking about. Letting them know that you are giving them your full attention is going to help the conversation go much more smoothly. You need to really extend the efforts to make sure that you're speaking calmly and respectfully to your partner and keeping the empathy in your heart and in your words. The best way to have a calm conversation where something might actually get accomplished is to speak in a way that is not going to make your partner feel attacked. Remember that when you're speaking empathy to each other, you are making sure that you are trying to let them know that you are extending the effort to make this work and by not letting your anger get the best of you the conversation will go a lot smoother or and communication will be much more effective.

A good thing to remember about speaking emphatically with your partner is to think about something very important. If you wouldn't speak a certain way with others, why would you speak that way with your partner? If you wouldn't be cruel in your speech with your mother or a friend, why would you speak that way to the person that means the most to you? Thinking about it like this should make you realize that you don't want to and that you shouldn't. You need to be honest with yourself and your partner, yes. However, you need to be kind when you do it. If you talk to couples they will tell you that you have to be honest is the number one thing that you need for your relationship, but they will also tell you that speaking kindly is the number one thing that you should remember. You can still speak honestly while practicing empathic dialogue; you just have to understand how not to hurt your partner. It is important to remember, though that you don't have to hurt their feelings when you do this.

One of the things that can benefit your empathetic dialogue is doing it intentionally and with purpose. What this means is that you show concern and care for your partner and express gratitude for what they do. When speaking to your mate, be sure to share your feelings openly and don't be afraid. Speak to your mate and tell them that it's alright to sit with each other's feelings so that you two can work through them together. When you're speaking to them, be sure that your remembering to listen emphatically as well because they will be sharing their innermost feelings and thoughts with you and that deserves respect.

Be intentional when you're asking your partner to be empathetic and talk to you. have them actually sit down and talk with you face to face. Remember that though it may be hard, you need to make sure that sarcasm and criticism are not in this conversation. If your upset be constructive instead of hostile. Your partner is obviously not going to respond to you in the way that you want, and the only thing that you are doing is creating unnecessary blocks that are going to damage your relationship. Instead of hurting each other, you should intentionally spend time together and try to cultivate a lasting connection instead. If you're stuck talking to each other tell your partner the truth so that the two of you can begin to fix the issue together.

Another thing that should be remembered about empathetic speaking is that you are not just trying to understand your partner's pain you're also trying to acknowledge their pain and let them know that you are genuinely aware of what they are experiencing. When someone is feeling pain, it is honestly very rare that a response can actually make the situation better or make them feel better. What actually makes the situation better is the connection that you have with your partner and how you feel about each other. Show them that you care and speak to them in a way that lets them know that if you are not only understanding exactly what they're going through and what they think but that you're acknowledging them and letting them know that even if you don't have the answer you're there for them. Just being there for them is going to strengthen your connection in a way that you haven't even thought of before. Empathetic dialogue isn't just for when things are going well. You need to be able to speak with empathy when things are rough and you're going through hard times as well — being able to show your partner that you care enough to listen to what they have to say and that your acknowledging the situation that they've been put in is enough to make them realize that you're speaking to them with empathy and understanding.

When you're putting yourself in your partner's shoes and letting them know that you get them you can ask them what they would do. If you don't understand the situation, then ask them. This is a really good way to develop your empathy skills and how you can use them to improve how you speak. It's also, unfortunately, the least used way to develop your emphatic skills. It's fine if you can't figure out what the other person wants and it's also just as ok to ask them and have them tell you. Remember you don't get a medal for trying to figure out everything on your own and if you need some help to understand your partner should appreciate the fact that you care enough to ask in the first place so that you can try to make the situation better for them.

You should practice these skills with your partner so that your connection and your bond become more unified. When you practice these skills, you will be able to be a more caring and compassionate person as well as being more approachable, which means that your partner will be able to approach you easier. This is really going to help your relationship because when couples experience a communication breakdown, their relationship suffers because they feel as if they don't understand each other. Making yourself approachable for your mate is so beneficial because your partner will be able to talk to you more freely and be more at ease.

This is a great gift that you would be giving your partner, and it's a great gift that you would be giving your relationship. It also benefits you because it will help you be able to speak in your daily life as well. If you're trying to develop an empathetic dialog with your partner, then you need to listen carefully and make a note of the phrases and keywords that your partner is using with you in the conversations that you are having. You need to pay attention mentally and physically to what's happening so that you know how to respond in a way that doesn't hurt your partner or what you're trying to achieve.

When you do respond to the conversation, you should respond with encouragement and kindness to the message that your partner is trying to tell you. Just as it is hard for you to speak with him, sometimes, it would be just as hard for him to speak to you. Often in a relationship, you might find that the fear of what to say holds you back from what you actually want to say. You shouldn't let this affect your relationship, and instead, you should try to move past it for the sake of communication and for the sake of your relationship. Remember that you should never be afraid to speak to your partner and say what you really need to say. They love you, and you love them, so you need to make sure that you are open to having a conversation with them. If when you're having a conversation, your partner's feelings and thoughts change, then you should remember that you can change yours as well. You should remember that flexibility is a very important part of being able to have an empathetic dialogue. This is honestly one of the most significant efforts that you can make toward improving your skills and communication with your partner. When you are able to understand your partner through working on your empathetic dialogue skills, he will want to understand you in return, and it will be easier for him to do so. This is how you start to heal communication skills as well as being able to work on your collaboration and your team work together as a couple.

CHAPTER 3: HOW TO APPRECIATE YOUR PARTNER AND ACCEPT THEM FOR WHO THEY ARE

In any relationship, we need to be able to accept our partners the way they are no one is perfect and an important thing to remember is that perfection is a myth. No one in this world is perfect, and everyone is flawed. If you come into your relationship thinking that your partner is perfect and that you won't have any issues then this you are setting yourself up for very unrealistic expectations. Surprisingly many enter their relationships with that exact thought in mind and then can't understand why they have issues later on. It's because they didn't realize that chasing perfection doesn't get you anywhere. Instead of trying to make everything perfect, accept your partner how they are, and love them unconditionally.

When we decide to share our life with someone else we've already taken the time to get to know them, and we take the time to understand who they are and what they're about when we take the step to join our lives with them forever we have told them that we accept them for who they are Is after you have gotten in a relationship you find that this is not true anymore than your relationship needs work a relationship cannot work if you do not accept your partner for who they are By that same logic by that same logic your partner and yourself will have bed communication and find that you're unable to communicate as efficiently as you'd like to because you feel that your partner doesn't understand you which can lead to feelings of neglect.

Remember that you don't want your partner to have unrealistic expectations of you so you shouldn't have unrealistic expectations for them either. If you want your relationship to work, then you will need to understand the importance of being able to make sure that you are thinking realistically.

When you become frustrated with your partner, you need to pull back and recognize what it is you're thinking. Is what you are thinking something that your partner really needs to change or is it something that you've built up in your mind because you have unrealistic expectations about what they should be or what you want them to be? Is it something that you need to change with your thought process, or is it something that genuinely needs to be changed in your partner himself? Another question that you should ask yourself is why is it your partner's job to live up to unrealistic expectations? On the opposite side to this, why is it your job to live up to your partner's unrealistic expectations? You need to realize that having the right expectations of yourself, your partner, and your relationship are the best ways that you're going to be able to make this relationship work.

Flexibility is another thing that is going to help you appreciate your partner and make sure that you are accepting them the way they are. It's very easy to think of the world as just black or just white and think that this is wrong, or this is right, and there is no in-between, but that's not realistic. Things don't have to be one way or the other. Instead of labeling your way as the right way or your partner's way is the right way, remember that you need to compromise and understand how things actually are.

Negative thinking is much easier for some people than positive thinking because being negative doesn't require half as much effort as being positive. When a person is being negative and thinking negatively, it's very self-imposed and self-centered behavior. When we think negatively, we are not accepting our partner for who they are, and instead, you see the negative in them because you're focusing on being negative yourself. Being positive instead of focusing on why your partner is the way that he is will cause you to be able to focus on what's amazing about him and why you like him in the first place. This, in turn, is going to lead you to accept him for who he is, and this will lead to you appreciating him for who he is as well. Just as you need the love of your partner to make you happy and whole, your partner needs your love to make him happy and whole as well. He needs you to be here for him as well.

Another helpful hint to appreciating your partner is to force yourself to see things in a different light and put the focus on you. What we mean by this is that you should ask yourself how you would feel if your partner was judging you the way that you're judging them. Another question you should ask is that if they didn't accept you the way that you're not accepting them how you would feel if you thought your partner didn't understand you or love you the way that you needed to be loved and respected? Keeping this in mind, you'll be much more flexible, and you'll be able to understand why you shouldn't treat your partner this way.

You should also strive to remember that the past is gone and there's nothing you can do about it. You can make up for the past. That part is possible, and we're not saying that it is not. What we're saying is whatever happened in the past you can't go back in time and make it so that that didn't happen. There are no do-overs or a reset button on the things you do because life is not a video game. It's here and now and you need to learn that if you make a mistake, you can't undo it, but you can try and fix it and move on from it. You just need to remember that whatever has happened has already happened and there's nothing you can do to change that. We all make mistakes, so instead of focusing on the past, try living in the present and give your partner the gift of understanding that. If you're always comparing things to how they were before or you're always comparing things to the past and bringing up past arguments along with things that can't be changed, the only thing that you are actually doing is hindering your acceptance of your partner and your acceptance of each other. If this continues over time, it could actually end up destroying your relationship because you're not focusing on the future the way that you need to be. The biggest reason that this is an issue that can be so damaging is because when you are doing this, it brings resentment and past pain to the relationship. This, in turn, brings hurt into the relationship, along with fighting and harsh words. To avoid this, you should focus on the present and what you can do in the present to change things to make them better for your partner and yourself.

When we judge others it's often a result of our own personal criticisms that we've had to endure ourselves, but we shouldn't put pressure on ourselves to do things a certain way, and we shouldn't put pressure on our partner to do things that way either. Letting what others have said to you or done to you can affect you and your thought process and the way you treat others, including your partner. This is why people say your past shapes who you are. If your mistreated when your younger or you've had bad relationships you can unintentionally carry that over into your future relationships even though you don't mean to. The way to get past this is to understand that that is what you've got this issue in the first place and then work on trying to change. In the long run, this will ensure that your heart and spirit are happier and more fulfilled. This will cause your treatment of your partner to get better and make sure that your partner's spirit and heart are happier too.

When you put unnecessary pressure on your partner, the only thing you're doing is pushing them away. Now every relationship has pressure, and every relationship has areas where your partner will be under pressure but what we're saying is instead of judging yourself and judging others understand that everyone has limitations and you can't put too much pressure on someone because they will crack. This may not happen right away, especially if your partner is strong, but eventually, even the strongest person can break eventually if you keep pushing them too hard. If you cause your partner to crack, then your relationship is going to falter immediately because they're going to feel resentment towards you for doing so. When you are happy and fulfilled as an individual you will be less critical and rude to your partner.

Something to remember is that even though your partner can meet your needs, you can meet your own needs as well. You can also meet your partner's needs as they meet yours. In order to fully appreciate your partner and to accept them for who they are, you need to remember that when you are happy with yourself, you'll be happy with everything around you. The same is true if you're unhappy. If you are unhappy with everything around you, you are going to be overly critical of your partner, and you won't appreciate them for who they are.

When you recognize that you're unhappy, you will at least be able to understand that you need to tell your partner in a loving and respectful manner that you're unhappy. Then you can work together on becoming happier so that you can appreciate each other and accept each other the way you need to. Negativity in a relationship is one of the biggest reasons that a relationship can falter because when that happens, it breeds insecurity, painful arguments, and hurt in the relationship that you have. When you're able to understand that you and your partner can meet your needs and that you should apply positive thinking instead of negativity, you'll be able to see your partner as your partner. This is what you should be seeing them as instead of just seeing your partner as someone who's supposed to meet every single need of yours.

Something to remember is that a happy relationship will occur when two people are happy and content. When two people are happy and content with coming together and being together, they realize that their relationship has fewer problems and they are much better at appreciating each other. Many people have heard the expression that their partner completes them, and for many, this is true. For just as many, they feel completely alone and love that that feeling grows with their partner. For many happy couples, they understand that they feel complete already with their partner and with themselves. So they have the best of both worlds.

Each of us has to be responsible at least in part for our own happiness and because of this happy person in a relationship is able to increase the flexibility and the happiness that you have together as a couple in your relationship. Flexibility is very important when accepting your partner for who he is. This is because when you're able to be flexible is the ability to see that you can converse with your partner freely and without judgment. It also helps your ability to be able to compromise in your relationship.

You never want to hurt your partner or be cruel to them, and you need to remember that this is why you need to remember the tips of empathetic dialogue as well as listening in the same way. The way that we speak with our partners can affect every part of our relationship, and if you want to have your partner feel like you appreciate them for who you are, then you will need to make sure you watch your words. You can speak to your partner and tell them what you need to say, but there is a proper way to do it, and you shouldn't be cruel and unkind.

Remember that your partner has good qualities. You wouldn't have a relationship with your partner if you didn't like them. That means that when your angry and frustrated, you need to remember that there are things that you love about your partner. The next time you think to yourself, 'I can't believe my partner did this, he's awful' or something that is along with those same stop yourself. Remind yourself of your partner's good qualities instead. Think of how your partner is loving and kind or how he's a good provider and is always there for you. This puts your mind in a different headspace and takes the anger away. Then you can have a civilized conversation and remember that anger isn't what's going to make your partner feel loved.

If you have a faith-filled relationship, then a big way that you can let your partner know that they are loved and appreciated is to remember how the Bible describes a healthy, loving relationship. Your partner is the person that you have the most intimate relationship with, and you need to love them completely and practice patience and kindness. A faith-filled relationship requires that you put your selfishness, arrogance, and pride away. The same is true for unforgiveness and tempers. You need to stop thinking of yourself and think of your partner as well. This will lead you to feel loved and appreciated, but it will also let your partner feel the same way. This is what a relationship needs. Acceptance is a key part of any relationship. Once you are able to feel the acceptance and love for each other, you can begin to feel completely comfortable being your true self. When people feel accepted, and they don't feel judged instead of closing themselves off to their love, they will open up instead because they are not worried about negative consequences. They are not worried about your judgment because they feel accepted and safe.

Let your differences complement each other instead of letting them hurt you. No matter how similar you are in your relationship, you will still have differences. Instead of trying to change your partner or have them try to change you, understand that your differences aren't a bad thing. They can complement you, and they don't have to cause a barrier or a problem for you. Your partner doesn't have to like dancing just because you do or the same television shows. You don't have to hate that your partner doesn't. Let your differences make you stronger and accept that they can work with you and not against you.

A good story for learning how to accept your partner and how it can help you is a woman was irritated with her partner and couldn't stand some of the things about him that made him who he was. Then she developed cancer. The things that had bothered her before were now the things that she needed and liked about him because it was helping her get through this awful time in her life. His ability to be direct in his communication came in handy when they were dealing with the doctors, and she found that she wasn't upset at his quirks anymore but pleased and very grateful because it took the weight off of her. She realized that when she was able to accept her partner for who he was full, she was happier in her relationship. She was also able to realize that she and her partner were able to build a healthier relationship and a long-lasting one. As she accepted her partner, he, in turn, accepted her and they were able to solidify their relationship into something much stronger. This is a great testament to what can happen when your ability to love and accept your partner as they are.

CHAPTER 4: HOW TO BE YOURSELF NATURALLY

In any part, if life it is important for you to be yourself and it is very important in a relationship. If you can't be yourself in your relationship, then you have a serious issue. Your partner needs to see you. If your hiding who you really are, then your partner never knows you. Why then would you stay in a relationship with someone who doesn't truly know you? The answer is simple. You would want a solution. No one wants to stay in a situation where they feel like they don't know their partner.

Some important reasons that being yourself are so important in a relationship are so that your partner can get to know the real you. If your partner doesn't know the real you then they can feel deceived, hurt, and feel like they're in a relationship with someone who is a fraud or who doesn't understand them at all. They could also feel as if they don't know you at all and everything that they have built this relationship to be a lie. Like you haven't told the truth in any aspect. Another reason this is so important is that your partner wants to know the real you - not an idea of you or a fake persona that you may be using. They want to love you and all of you just the way you are. You should want to be able to be yourself for your partner as well.

When we are hiding who we are and are not acting like ourselves, we begin to put up a fake persona and have people think that is the real us. Like the people that make-believe they have a great life on Instagram or Twitter. They make their relationship look perfect though it is fake. An interesting thing to note is that hiding yourself can come from fear. The fear is of being able to speak or fear of showing who we really are. When you're trying to communicate in a relationship with your partner, the communication is stifled when you're too afraid to say what you really want to say or you're too afraid to show who you really are. This fear can keep you from recognizing your true self, but it can also severely impact your relationship and the trust and unity the two of you have together. As this would be affecting the communication in your relationship, the communication would break down. As the communication breaks down because of this fear and because you're not honest, your relationship will falter.

A true connection in a relationship should have you and your partner being real with each other. When you can't do this, you keep your partner at arm's length, and you have to hide how you feel and what you want out of your life. Your partner can't relate to you because he doesn't know you. We have spoken about why practicing empathy and why it is important for communication. Being your true self gives your partner the opportunity to relate to you and understand how your feeling. Without being able to relate to you, he can't do this.

What you need to do for yourself and for your relationship is to be yourself. Your natural self. If you can do this, then your relationship will have the ability to have a relationship that won't be mired in fear and manipulation but trust and love. In order to learn how to be yourself, you need to understand how special you are.

You are a special person, and the first thing you need to do is to be able to remember that every day. You have something inside you that makes you different from everyone else around you. This is a great thing! Imagine how boring life would be if we were all the same. You have your own strengths and feelings that makeup who you are. Living as yourself means that your happy with who you are and realizing that you don't have anything to hide and that you can be yourself. A great gift that you would be able to give yourself is to be yourself simply. When you are able to open yourself up to the possibility of being you and learning that you don't have to be afraid, once you are able to get past the fear, you can see that you will be able to learn the strengths that you have, and you will be able to see that your relationship will be able to have a greater chance of succeeding because your bond will be gaining strength as you do.

One of the best tips that you can utilize for figuring out who you are is to journal. You should ask yourself what you love to do and what makes you happy? Everyone has passions and gifts that make you special. What are you good at and what makes you feel like you have hope? When do you think about the person that you want to be, what do you see? Another big question to ask, what is your purpose? What do you want people to see when they look at you?

By journaling and learning who you are through your own words, you will begin the process of understanding who you are. Something to consider, as this does happen in certain cases if your partner is not responding positively to you being yourself know that they can be happy with it and that in the long run, this is better because you're coming from a place of strength rather than emptiness.

The less threatened you feel in your relationship, the easier it is to be able to be yourself in your relationship. You and your partner need to be open to the idea of changing if the both of you need to for the sake of your relationship and each other. Boundaries in a relationship also make it easier for you to be your natural self. If you realize that you're not your true self, the first thing that you need to do is be aware of it and then realize that things need to change. This is going to be another major part of being able to be yourself.

Even in a relationship, you still need time for yourself, and this doesn't make you a bad partner to your partner or a bad partner to your partner. Think about when your partner gets off work. He needs a few minutes to himself before he's ready to talk about his day and connect with you, right? This isn't because he's a jerk, it's because he needs a few moments to recharge for himself. You would need the same after a long day at work, and it's the same concept. When you get time to yourself, use the time to reflect and think about things. You will see that you do miss your partner, who is a good thing, but you will be taking the time for yourself, which is what you need for you.

You should also have a hobby that's your own. It is amazing if you share a lot of the same interests and hobbies as your partner, but you should also have a hobby that allows you to things on your own. Doing things on your own is another thing that you need to do for yourself because this is going to lead to a balance in your relationship. You're still a unique individual that has different wants and tastes than your partner and doing something on your own is a great way to discover who you are if you haven't already. This is also going to help your relationship at the same time.

Going out with your friends or your family can be a really great thing to do for you and yourself as well. If you're not a social type of person, you can talk to people that you care about and that you like hanging out with. Your partner can also do this because they need to have time with their friends as well. If you desire to do this together, you may, but it's just as important that you do it for yourself as well. It's okay to have friends that are just yours.

You need to make sure that you love yourself as well. This is one of the most important tips. You can't truly be yourself if you arenno6 loving yourself. When you don't love yourself, you tend to hide who you really are and tell people what they want to hear. You shouldn't do that. Let them fall in love with the real you. This is going to ensure that you keep things in your life and in your relationship balanced. There is an old saying that says that nobody can love you unless you love yourself. So you need to remember that you have to like and take care of yourself as well as loving and taking care of your partner. Another saying that rings true says that it is way too hard to love another person when you can't even love yourself. For the sake of yourself and your relationship, you need to be able to really like and love yourself.

When you're in a relationship, another thing to remember is that it's not just your partner that can make you happy. You can make yourself happy too. If your partner feels threatened by you being independent or strong, then they're the ones that need to change. Even though you're in a relationship, you still need to make sure that you're able to maintain some independence. Honesty is one of the biggest things in any relationship, and you need to make sure that you're honest not only for yourself but for your partner as well. Not only to and for yourself but your partner as well. A great example of this for most people is moving in together or taking a big step in a relationship. Now obviously as you're in a relationship, you would already be living together, but this is just an example that most people face. If your partner had asked you to move in with him and you are not ready, you shouldn't act like you are. Instead, you should be honest and tell them that it's not the right move for you because it'll save you from heartache later. In a relationship, if your partner asks you something and you're not comfortable with it, or you're not ready, to be honest with them and be honest with yourself because if you're can't you're not going to be happy in your relationship.

Loving your partner and loving your relationship doesn't mean that they always get their way. You have your own thoughts and ideas, as well as your own wants. You don't need to agree with your partner on everything all of the time. If they're doing something that makes you uncomfortable or if there's even something that you don't like, you need to tell them. Compromise is a big part of the relationship, but it doesn't mean that you don't get to speak up for yourself and it doesn't mean that you don't get to tell your partner how you really feel. If you can be honest and understand that there is a difference between compromise and not having a voice at all, your relationship will come out better for it.

Respect is big in any relationship as well and if you can't respect yourself, how are you going to respect your partner? Respecting yourself is a key part of being able to accurately and honestly be yourself. If you feel like you are giving more than you can, this isn't healthy for your relationship, but it's also damaging to you and being able to feel any sense of self. You need to have an honest and open dialogue with your partner. If something is wrong, then you need to be able to have enough respect for your relationship and for yourself to tell your partner what is wrong.

Remember that no one is perfect. Don't try to be the perfect partner for your partner. Perfection is a myth, and many couples have hardships because they try to chase the impossible. You won't discover who you are chasing perfection. Admit that it's okay to make mistakes. You don't need to be anything other than yourself because your partner loves you for you are. No relationship is perfect, and if you are able to remember this than you will be able to have a good relationship and be proud of yourself for who you are. If you have done wrong, admit it and then understand and move on while making sure that you don't repeat that same mistake.

In understanding who you are, you should realize that there are things that you can do and things that you can't. You and your human need to accept that fact you have limitations. If there is something that you feel like you can't do, then you need to be honest about it and tell your partner that you can't do whatever it is your partner is asking of you. If you can do it, let your partner know, so that they know this is something that you're comfortable with. This makes it easier to understand what your limitations are and what your able to do and what you are not able to do. Pushing yourself too hard doesn't help your partner, and it doesn't help you. Show them that you have genuinely tried your best but don't hurt yourself trying to go to hard. Remember, if your partner truly loves you, they will understand that you are not perfect and that you have limitations. They will want to help you because of that same love.

Keep a good fitness routine. Many people say that when they are discovering who they are confident is a big part of discovering who they are. Just as many have said that fitness gave them a large boost in their confidence. One of the biggest ways that you can gain confidence is to do the things that are going to be able to build that confidence for you. Fitness also offers you mental benefits that help you discover who you are. When you begin to get healthier and feel better your mind improves which as well lets you have a more positive attitude and can help you be willing to discover who you are if this is something you've been struggling with this. You can receive focus, determination, focus, and clarity from becoming healthy as well, which will also help you on your journey of self-discovery.

Challenging yourself can also offer great benefits as well. Being able to push yourself and challenge yourself can offer a boost of confidence and push you outside of your comfort zone. Once you've begun to do this, the more success, you will have as well as gaining new skills and new virtues or thoughts. This is important to self-discovery. When we push ourselves toward something new, you can discover a whole new set of passions and interests that you didn't even know you had for yourself. By not challenging yourself, your relationship may be feeling stale, or you could find yourself unhappy. Avoid this and push yourself.

Something that can help you find out who you are is also to take charge of your mental health as well as your physical health. This is going to be able to help you in the long run because it changes how your attitude is. Working out is what will help you stay healthy physically, but it helps your mental health as well because you're more optimistic and you're stronger on a day to day basis, but you also need to focus on your mental health as well because your mental health plays a big part in who you are. If you realize that you need to do something for your mental health to be better, you need to be able to do it and explain to your partner that you're working on yourself as well as working on the relationship. Your partner should be able to understand out of the love that they have for you.

When we have a relationship, another thing that we need to look at is faith. For many people, their faith can be a big point of definition in who they are, and one of the ways that you can stay yourself in your relationship is to pray alone. Now, something that should be noted is that if you and your partner have the same faith or similar faith, you can use your faith as a point of connecting with each other and as a way to build the bond that the two of you need to have. However, individually you need different things, and you would have different things to pray for, so although you can pray with your partner, it can be spiritually fulfilling to pray by yourself as well. Both ways offer benefits. Most people need to be able to carve out just a quiet moment in their lives on a day to day basis, and if that's what you need as well, then that's perfectly fine. Once you realize that you're becoming closer to your faith, this can also be a great way to help you define who you are, and it can help you realize what you stand for. In many situations, the most important thing is that you take responsibility for your own spiritual life. When you feel like you're spiritually drained you may feel hopeless and depressed, but when you feel nourished with your faith you can be there for yourself, and you can be there for your partner if his faith is ever shaken.

Personal growth can help you learn who you are and help you to be who you are in your relationship as well. It can also help you find a new sense of self-worth, which allows you to see your relationship, yourself, and your partner with brand new eyes. When people invest in their own personal growth, they can find that they are claiming a part of themselves that they feel like they've lost. They can also reclaim a part of themselves that they haven't seen for a long time and it can allow them to find their own voice. You can also find your personal truths which will, in turn, find itself apart of your relationship. A good example of this is if you're paranoid in your relationship for whatever reason and you take the time to find your personal growth, you might find that you now know what you're worth and that you're not paranoid anymore because you know that you have no reason to be. Another example is that if you don't feel pretty enough and you invest in some self-growth, you will see that you are more than pretty. More than beautiful. You will see that you're amazing just the way you are and once you figure out who you are you'll be much happier because you won't have to guess what you're about or what makes you who you are. This is because you will know.

Resentment has no place in a relationship, and when you give yourself the opportunity to understand who you are and when you try to become the best version of yourself, you'll be more satisfied with your life. This, in turn, means that you won't have any more resentment. Following this, finding out who you are helps you take responsibility and ownership for your joy and your happiness, and in doing so, this puts an end toward all the resentment that you could have toward your partner, and you can realize what an incredible partner your partner actually is.

When you know yourself, and you're trying to be yourself in your relationship, you need to understand your own personality. When some people attempt to learn to find out who they are, they have no idea what their personality is. While this may seem like something that everybody should have a handle on some people really don't know their own personality, and this is going to create problems in a relationship because you have to be able to understand who you are fully. It also helps if after you find out who you are that you understand who your partner is, which is something that we have already covered in the previous chapter.

CHAPTER 5: UNDERSTANDING THE ART OF PERSUASION

Another thing that most people have heard of in relationships is the art of persuasion. One key thing that this book would like to make obvious if it wasn't already is that you should never use persuasion to manipulate your partner into doing something that they don't want to do, and you should never manipulate your partner in the first place. Many people have confused persuasion and manipulation, and they are not the same. Manipulation is the act of controlling or using someone and has negative connotations. They twist words and play on your emotions to get what they want from you. Persuasion is you trying to get your partner to agree with you or see your side of things; however, it is not the art of manipulating your partner or belittling them. Instead, persuasion is where you are making an argument for why you believe you are right and then presenting your case.

This is why coercive tactics which are usually of the belittling nature and make fun of your partner simply for disagreeing with you and displaying their own opinion is not what we're trying to do. You should instead you should use logic and reasoning using factual information and logic to help your partner understand where you're coming from. That would be in the art of persuasion that does not hurt your partner and can strengthen your relationship because it helps your partner see your side instead of trying to coarse them or forcing them to do what you want them to do. That would fall under the category almost of blackmail and blackmail is not something that you want in a relationship either. When you have blackmail or coercion in a relationship the first things that can happen is the breeding of resentment, distrust, hurt and it can cause the end of a relationship if it gets too far out of hand.

For the importance of a relationship, you could reference relationship tactics. This is where you are explaining shared relationship outcomes or appealing to your partner's love or concern. Instead of using statements that use the word 'I,' you need to use statements like "us". Relationship referencing tactics are usually the most persuasive for both women and men because each part of the tactics appeals to each partner. When both partners feel like they have a close romantic relationship, then they will be moved by the love, understanding, and care that they have for their partner. Another persuasion tactic is logic and reasoning. This tactic is hit or miss. Logic and reasoning when studied have been proven to not really be affective or non-affective and in fact, sometimes they can prove to be counterproductive. It is however still healthier than coercive tactics which should never be used.

Many studies have shown that when you try coercive tactics on your partner it has the worst effects of other tactics and it actually drives your partner toward greater disagreement, greater arguing and in some cases, it can cause marital damage. Many studies have shown that referencing relationship tactics appear to work very well when you're trying to bring your mate around to what you're trying to think and what you're trying to explain to them instead of being passive-aggressive and hostile. You could explain why you think this would be the best choice for your relationship or use the following sentence. I am trying to explain something to you because I think that this would be the best choice for our relationship. Notice in the sentence above that it started using words like I, and that doesn't work but then look at the last part of the sentence and notice when she was trying to get her partner to come around to her line of thinking, she used the word ours. Remembering that the term our is what you should be utilized instead of I or me, she said our relationship and not my relationship or your relationship. When she said our relationship what she was doing was signifying that she was talking about the two of them together as one overall.

Most studies show that this creates a perception of both of you being similar instead of you being torn apart or dissimilar. This shows you together as a couple and in greater agreement with each other because of that. This is beneficial, and this should be what you want. You want to be two people united and similar instead of being in disagreement and two separate people. Remember that while you are two separate people when you marry, you become one. This means that your goal should be agreeing together. This is why you're persuading your partner in the first place.

During these efforts, most people tend to try and persuade their partner through loving thoughts, and they take a moment to be mindful of how special their relationship actually is. They also use this opportunity to remind their partner of how sacred their relationship is to them and how special it is to them. Another thing that they show their partner is what their relationship means to them. This is a great way to show your partner that you appreciate them and that they really mean something to you.

They also work on their conversation skills. Building good conversation skills are going to help you communicate with your mate much more effectively, and they're going to help you influence your partner more effectively as well. This is because you're bringing them around to your line of thinking. Remember however that you are not trying to force them to your line of thinking. If they genuinely disagree with you, you cannot force them to do what they don't want to do. What you are trying to do is show them what you're thinking and help them understand where you're coming from. Remember, in the previous chapters; we talked about empathetic listening and dialogue of the same nature. The reason that they come into play here is that you're trying to get your mate to see what you're thinking and understand you. Empathetic listening and dialogue will help here because those are the standards of both of those types of communication. They are designed to help partners feel understood, heard, and connected to each other in a deeper way.

Remember, when you are attempting to persuade your partner, you are going to need to use a mix of dialogue communication, and you will need to use your body language and nonverbal communication skills as well. If you are going to successfully convince someone of something or show them why you think they should agree with you on something you need to make sure that you are secure in yourself and why you think your right in the first place. You also need to need to make sure that you are using the posture and look of someone who is sure of what they are saying. Remember, you have something that you want your partner to agree with you about. This means that you need to be sure in yourself and why you want them to agree with you in the first place.

When you're attempting to persuade your partner, you need to remember that if logic and reasoning by themselves don't seem to work, then you should remember it's because humans are very emotional creatures. In addition to this, romantic relationships aren't just logical. They are emotional, as well. In this case, you should remember that you can ask your partner directly for what it is that you want and openly discuss it with them so that they understand what it is that you need from them and your relationship. The strategies for persuasion are most beneficial and effective if you use them in accordance with the relationship tactics from above.

There are other tips that people use for the art of persuasion that is effective as well. Repetition is a component of the art of persuasion because most people today have developed ways of ignoring things and don't understand them or focus on them until at his been told to them several times or have seen it many times such as in a text message or a messenger text. There is an issue with this, however. Many partners don't appreciate having to repeat themselves ten or fifteen times. It makes them feel like you don't care.

Another tool in the art of persuasion is to personalize your message to match what you're wanting. An example here is if you're approaching an investor or a customer you would need to listen to them first to find a personal area of interest with whatever idea it is that you've come up with. If the person that you're talking to is creative, then you shouldn't use logic and analytical components with them. This is true for a partner, as well. Instead, you should establish a relationship and go from there. This is where a partner differs. When it concerns your partner, you already have a relationship, so instead of using logic and reasoning to help form a relationship, you should use the relationship communication skills along with logic and reasoning.

When using the ideas of logic and reasoning, you should present the evidence of the best case you can possibly have. Make sure that you do the research needed and that you have solid proof of why you're right and why your partner should listen to you or change their mind in the end.

Convincing someone of why you need to be right is going to need the most convincing evidence possible, especially if your partner tends to be on the stubborn side. Your partner will want to work with you and understand you if they can see for themselves that you've created a strong case and that you know what you're talking about. This also helps because even if they are stubborn, it's hard to argue with factual evidence that's staring you right in the face. It's also hard to argue with analytic evidence staring you in the face. Another thing to make sure of is that you're not talking without thinking. Many arguments have actually started because of the fact that people tend to talk without thinking first. Be sure that you've made an effort and your side of the argument without being hostile.

Another tool in your arsenal for persuasion is to understand how to connect with your partner. Studies have shown that when people feel connected to you, they're much more likely to accept what you have to say. When you are connecting with your partner, be sure not to act is if your partner is a target. This is very important, and it needs to be remembered. Your partner is not your target and doesn't need to be treated as a target. They need to be treated with the love and respect that they deserve as your partner.

You need to connect with them on a personal level and a deeper level. If you cannot do that, then the chances are that your partner is going to doubt everything you say and that they're not going to believe you. When you're trying to establish your point, and you're using the art of persuasion. Another thing that you'll need to remember is not to push too hard. Persuasive people are not aggressive, and they are not pushy. Pushy people are a massive turn off for many people, and no one really likes in your face approach. This usually makes people backpedal right away because they feel like they're being attacked. That's not what you want.

If you're trying to persuade your partner to see your point, you should remember that persuasive people don't argue like regular people. In fact, they don't really argue at all because they recognize that that isn't going to get them anywhere. They realize that being subtle is what's going to win them the argument. However, they're not overly mousy either. They don't push too hard or go to soft. What they try to do is fall somewhere in the middle. They present their ideas to the best of their ability, and they make sure that they have the attention of the person that they're trying to connect to.

This is what you need to do for your partner. You don't need to be overly mousy and soft-spoken, but you don't need to be overly pushy, aggressive and hostile to the point where he runs in the opposite direction as fast as his feet can carry him either. Follow the example of the persuasive people and see if you can reach that happy middle ground in between. We said earlier that your body language is also going to come into play here and it is important you give it some thought.

When you utilize positive non-verbal communication, it can include quality to the verbal messages or thoughts that you need to pass on, and help you to abstain from sending blended or befuddling signals. In this segment, we'll portray some essential stances that you can embrace to extend fearlessness and transparency.

1. Establishing a Confident First Connection
These tips can assist you in adjusting your non-verbal communication so you establish an extraordinary first connection:

Have an open stance. Be loose, however, don't slump! Sit or stand upstanding and place your hands by your sides. Avoid from remaining with your hands on your hips, as this will cause you to seem bigger, which can impart hostility or a longing to command.

Utilize a confident handshake. Nevertheless, don't escape! You don't need it to wind up unbalanced or, more awful, difficult for the other individual. If it does, you'll likely appear to be inconsiderate or forceful.

Keep up great eye-to-eye connection. Attempt to maintain eye contact with the other person for a couple of moments at once. This will demonstrate to her that you're true and locked in. Be that as it may, abstain from transforming it into a gazing match!

Stop making moves around your face. There's a typical observation that individuals who contact their appearances while responding to questions are being exploitative. While this isn't in every case genuine, it's ideal to avoid from tinkering with your hair or contacting your mouth or nose, especially if your point is to appear to be dependable.

Ponder how much an individual can pass on with only an outward appearance. A grin can demonstrate endorsement or satisfaction. A glare can flag objection or misery. At times, our outward appearances may uncover our actual sentiments about a specific circumstance. While you state that you are feeling fine, the expression all over may tell individuals generally.

Only a couple of instances of feelings that can be communicated through outward appearances include:

Happiness

Misery

Outrage
Shock

Nauseate

Dread

Confusion

Fervor

Want

Hatred

The appearance on an individual's face can even assistance decide whether we trust or accept what the individual is stating. One examination found that the most reliable outward appearance included a slight raise of the eyebrows and a slight grin. This articulation, the specialists recommended, passes on both cordiality and certainty.

Outward appearances are likewise among the most all-inclusive types of non-verbal communication. The articulations used to pass on dread, outrage, bitterness, and satisfaction are comparable all through the world.

Scientist Paul Ekman has discovered help for all-inclusiveness of an assortment of outward appearances attached to specific feelings including euphoria, outrage, dread, shock, and sadness.

Research even recommends that we make decisions about individuals' knowledge dependent on their countenances and articulations. One examination found that people who had smaller appearances and progressively conspicuous noses are bound to be seen as savvy. Individuals with grinning, blissful articulation are likewise decided to be keener than those with furious articulations.
The eyes are regularly alluded to as the "windows to the spirit" since they are equipped for uncovering a lot about what an individual is feeling or thinking. As you take part in discussion with someone else, observing eye

developments is a characteristic and significant piece of the correspondence procedure. Some regular things you may notice incorporate whether individuals are looking or turning away their look, the amount they are flickering, or if their students are enlarged.

The tone of your voice is very important here because it sets the mood, and it's going to help be one of the factors that make your argument solid. Making the tone of your voice positive and your body gestures and expressions positive as well is going to engage your partner rather than turn them away.

By making sure that your voice is enthusiastic your telling your partner that you are trying to make sure that your attracting your partner's attention and keeping it. Other tips that you should make sure of is that you're maintaining your eye contact. When you maintain eye contact, you're drawing your partner into you.

This is a good thing because this makes them more open and receptive to what you're saying. We are going for positive body language here not negative, so be sure that you are not crossing your arms as this is a classic sign of aggression. You should also lean toward the other person as this is showing them that you're really engaged in the conversation. If you want them to listen to you and come around to your side, this is going to help make sure that you keep their attention.

Positive body language will engage your partner and convince your partner you're saying something that they need to hear. This is another reason that you want to engage your partner. If you lose them halfway through talking to them, you're not going to be able to get them to finish listening to you. An additional tip that is a good idea is making sure that the information you're presenting to them is completely valid. Another thing to remember is when it comes to persuasion how you say something can be just as important as what you're trying to say. Make sure that your focusing on both.

Persuasive people are also able to communicate clearly, quickly, and effectively. When you have an idea of what you want to talk about actually talking about what you want your partner to agree with you about is fun and can be very easy to explain. This is especially true if you are attempting to make someone understand you. A good strategy here is to be well aware of your subject and make sure that you would be able to explain it to anyone. When you're explaining it, even the simplest mind should be able to understand what you're talking about. If you can, explain yourself effectively to someone who has an absolutely no idea what you are talking about and to people that have no background information on the subject or anything of that nature then you can make a persuasive case with your partner.

Another thing that is essential to being persuasive is that you need to be honest and genuine. There is not a single person on Earth who like someone who is fake. It makes people angry and hurts people when they find out that people they have trusted are fake and that someone wasn't being a real friend. People gravitate instead toward those who are genuine and honest. This is because when a person is genuine and honest, other people know they can trust them.

Concentrate on what is driving this conversation and what makes you happy, and then you are going to be able to be much more interesting. When you're trying to persuade people to your point, you need to remember that flexibility is something that can help you. Another thing that you will need is to be able to admit that you're not perfect. If your argument isn't perfect either, and you can admit to it, this is going to show your partner that you are open-minded and willing to listen to other people as well as listening to yourself.

Instead of stubbornly sticking to your case if you're wrong, admit that you can be wrong. You want your partner to remember and know that you have their best interests at heart. You want them to think thoughts along the lines of 'this makes a lot of sense,' and 'wow you really know what you're talking about.' What you don't want is for them to think thoughts like 'she so stubborn she's never going to acknowledge what I'm thinking' or 'she's pigheaded and bullheaded.' What you want them to know is that you're actively listening to what they have to say and that you're not just trying to force your opinion on them. Persuasive people also allow other people to be entitled to their own opinions, and they treat their opinions as valid. They do this out of respect for the person that they are talking to.

Persuasive people are also very good at asking the important questions. The biggest mistake that most people make when it comes to listening is that they fail to hear what's actually being said because they're so focused on what they're going to say next or how they want the person to respond to what they're saying. When you do that the words don't come out as clear, they come out loud and rushed. Once this happens, you lose all meaning, and you'd lose your audience as well. If you want to avoid this what you should do is ask questions. People will realize that you're listening and you're able to clarify what you're saying and can help your partner if they don't understand. You will be completely surprised at how much respect you can gain by showing your partner that you're listening and that you're asking questions to make sure that they can understand what you are talking about as well.

Bring your argument to life by being able to capitalize on knowing how to paint a picture. The best storytellers paint a picture with their words, and it makes their readers eat up their stories like hotcakes. You can follow their example and use your words to do the same. Show them what you're talking about and create a good story that puts your partner in the mindset of exactly what you're talking about so that they have no questions as to what it is you're trying to tell them.

They also know when to pull back. This is going to help you when you're trying to test out how persuasive you can be.

Urgency is a threat, and when you're trying to persuade people of something don't force people to agree with you right away. If you do that they're more likely to stand by their original opinion and not want to listen to you at all. Your impatience on trying to get them to listen to you is actually going to cause the opposite to happen because they're not going to want to listen to you because of your attitude. If they think you're pushy and think that you're rude, it's not going to matter how good your ideas are. They won't want to listen. Good ideas are often difficult to process right away, and if you're patient, your partner will be grateful because they will be fully aware of what it is you're trying to get them to agree to.

Persuasive people tend to be pleasers as well. Have you ever heard the expression 'you may lose the battle, but you're going to win the war'? Persuasive people have heard this expression, and as such, they never try to win a battle and then lose the war. They're going to win that battle, and in turn, they will win that war. They know when to stand their ground, but they also know when to pull back and make a sacrifice that will help their cause. If they know that their argument has flaws, they will pull back and make sure that you see that they're not trying to push you into something that you're not sure about. They will give in and give ground because they know that it's going to help them in the long run. Persuasive people do this because they know in the long run you're going to be able to win your case. By showing how flexible you are, you're going to be winning your partner over and then you win the argument.

Other helpful tips of persuasion that can help you when you're trying to convince your partner of something is that you should always remember that you're not just listening to yourself. You need to listen to your partner as well, or they will tell you that they don't care about what you have to say because they are going to feel like you don't care. Automatically this hurts your chances of getting him to listen to you when you're trying to get him on your side.

It's not just about you. It's also about what you have to do for them and what you can do for them. Remember that you're the one who is trying to convince them of something, not the other way around. Make sure that you're showing them that your willing to be patient and that you can respect and listen to them as well as you can.

To get them to want to listen to you in the first place, you should repeat their words back to them throughout the conversation. Repeating people's words back to them shows that you did listen to them and what they had to say. Another thing that it shows them is that you cared enough about the conversation to be able to repeat the conversation back. No one wants to feel as if you're not really interested and you don't really care.

Appreciation and love are two important things in any relationship but especially in a relationship. For your partner and the love you bear them, you should also show your appreciation and your respect for the person in front of you when you are speaking to them. You don't have to be a suck-up to do this because they won't believe you. People can tell when it's not real. Instead of being fake and just blowing smoke show them honest praise and honest appreciation.

When you are attempting to persuade someone to get them to see your side of it you should also understand that if you've made a mistake, you don't just have to admit that you're wrong, you should apologize. Apologizing and letting them know that you respect them enough to give them an apology is an important part of this is well. It shows maturity and reflection, which can also help your communication because your partner sees you as a mature companion for them. We already discussed that no one has to be right all the time, but we haven't discussed that when you do something wrong that you should apologize and let them know. This is an important step though because if they had done something to you that was wrong, then you would want an apology as well.

Use your partner's name. Your partner's name is an important part of his identity, and you can show love and respect for it by making sure that you remember that it is an important part of the language that's being used and that coming from the person that they love it can be a sign of affection and sweetness. This should be able to help them connect with you more even if they're mad at you; this would be able to help the connection on some level.

Gratitude is another thing they can help you with this. People are much more likely to reply to you if you're polite and you make sure that you're using your manners. Your partner would appreciate it as well because you're talking to him and treating him with the respect and love that he deserves as your mate.

Lead your argument with a question. As you're trying to persuade your partner to your side of the argument and your point of view it may be tempting to give away all the facts right away but try to get them to listen to you first. Make the argument mysterious and curious. When something is mysterious people are more invested because you've hooked them into your argument. You need to hook your partner on to what you're trying to say so throw a question out there first that will be able to make your partner eat every single word that you say and want to know more.

When your partner speaks, don't interrupt them. This is hard if you really want to talk, but you need to realize that they need to talk to. This is a partnership, and even though you're wanting to persuade them to do something that you're wanting, you still have to remember that they are your partner and they have opinions that need to be expressed as well. Even through persuasion, you can still hold a conversation with them and listen to what they have to say as well.

If you want to make sure that they're listening to you, let them speak and say their fill even if they run on and on. Let them continue to speak until they said everything that they need to say. Once they are done, you can speak again and continue with what you were saying.

The word yes is also another persuasive word and many people attempting to persuade people to use it often as they know the benefits that it provides. The word yes shows that you're acknowledging the other person and that you're admitting that they have a valid point of view as well. It doesn't mean that you're giving up your point to agree with theirs. It simply means that you've found another tool in your arsenal to use for yourself and that you can make your point easier by utilizing it. To say yes in a persuasive argument is to help you get your point across in a constructive way what isn't passive-aggressive or hostile.

Remember to keep your cool. Everything that we have learned so far has been about making sure that you are speaking and listening with empathy and that you are loving, kind, and respectful to your partner. The adage treats people the way you want to be treated rings very true. You need to make sure that you and your partner are both in this and treating yourselves the best that you can to improve your bonds of matrimony and unity.

Getting angry is only going to undo all the work that you're doing to make your relationship and your connection better. You can't communicate with each other effectively if you're both too angry to actually speak to each other logically and lovingly. When your angry and arguing not only are you not going to win the argument that you're trying to persuade to go your you're you are also causing pain and discontent in your relationship and depending on how far that goes, you could be causing lasting damage to your relationship that will need more repair and healing later on.

Think about it like this. Someone's behavior toward you can be completely unacceptable. They could get rude or make a few rude remarks to you as well as get angry at you. They might even try and make you lash out at them in return or say really mean things to you for no reason. When someone does this, it's very tempting to lash out and attack back because you feel attacked yourself. We get naturally defensive, and this causes more problems because once you on the defensive and there on the offensive, it can be hard to calm yourself down and have a civilized conversation.

In situations like this, many people don't stop and think, and they do lash out, but that comes with many negative consequences that you don't need. This is only going to cause problems for you and problems in your relationship. This doesn't have to happen, however. Remember the breathing technique and the tips for making sure that you're not losing your cool and that you stay calm and collected. Instead of lashing out what you need to do to get people to listen to you is to remain calm and hear what they have to say. Remember with our hearing being empathic it's easier for you to acknowledge that you understand what they're feeling and that you're trying to understand what they feel if you don't understand already. You should explain in this situation why you feel how you feel as well. This means that you need to explain to your partner why it is you do agree with what they're saying and why it is you don't agree with what they're saying if there is something that you do not agree with.

One thing that you need to make sure that you are able to remember is that you make sure that you're being honest about what you're saying. In this situation, you need to make sure that you're not lying, but you also need to make sure that you remember that everyone comes with baggage and that it's going to be a part of anyone you have a relationship with because no one is 100% innocent. No one understands why people act a certain way or do things the way that they do.

In order to understand them, you need to place yourself in their shoes. This is where the expression you never truly know how someone feels until you've walked a mile in their shoes. If you want to be persuasive in your argument then what you're going to have to do is make sure that you're not getting angry for no reason and utilizing these tips to stay calm and realize that you need to understand what your partner is going through in this particular moment.

People also need to realize something that most people don't, and that is to be successful when your persuading people is to give the people what they want. For this, to work, you need to understand what people want and then give it to them. People will give you what you want if you give them what they want. This is how business people make so much money. For example, Burger King makes millions because they realize what people want, and they keep coming out with delicious recipes to keep the masses buying their food. Companies like Nike and Oakley do the same. This is how they keep their customers so happy and have achieved multimillion-dollar success.

Learn from them for persuasion purposes and what is it that you truly want while finding out what people want at the same time. Find a way to give your partner to make them happy, and you will be able to win the argument. If you're trying to persuade him to do something, another thing to remember is what can you offer them as a benefit.

Humans are selfish; remember, many of them only want to do something if they can get something out of it in return. A great example that we are going to use here is something that many wives have an issue with in regard to their partner. The garbage. In this example, a partner wants her partner to take out the garbage, and he's left it alone for a week. This means that you've tried the ideas of repeating information and you've kept your cool and now your upset that it's still not taken out. One thing that might help it get done is to remember what we just said above. Human's want to know what's in it for them. In that case, tell him the benefits of him taking out the trash and why he should take it out the way she wants him too. Explain the benefit of taking out the garbage and why it's something that's so small and quick that it's inconsequential to argue about in the first place. If he wants to know what benefit he will get out of it, be sure to give him one.

Your patience is going to pay off when practicing the art of persuasion. This is a very delicate process, and the people who utilize it, and do it well are going to be able to know better than anyone that patience is key here. If your partner is saying no one day that doesn't mean that he will every day and that he won't change his mind later. It also doesn't mean that everyone else in your life is going to say no to you just because one person says no at the moment. One no doesn't mean that 500 other people won't say yes, but you also have to remember that it also starts with you. Confidence is the key to this, and the more you have, the bigger chance you have of succeeding with what you're trying to do.

CHAPTER 6: UNDERSTANDING THE IMPORTANCE OF PRACTICING EVERYDAY TO HAVE A MINDFUL RELATIONSHIP

In any relationship that you have in your life including the relationship that you have with yourself and the relationship that you have with your partner, your family, work, or any aspect of your life, you will want to practice being more mindful. Mindful relationships are going to be able to take you where you need to be and make sure that you're achieving all that you can. Mindful relationships are going to help you be able to be the best you can while making sure that you're happy in your relationship.

A happy relationship makes us feel more open and present, and while studies have shown that they are not completely accurate in saying that mindfulness produces relationship improvements, there have been a few studies that show that it might. Mindfulness helps people become more present and attentive in their relationships. Many people know how frustrating it can be to have to talk to your partner while they're constantly checking their phone, or their video games and their attention is always on something else when it should be on you.

It shouldn't matter if their mind is on work or if their mind is on friends, the point is that their mind is on something other than you. When you're acting and practicing a mindful relationship, and you're trying to be more mindful of your partner as well as yourself this changes the area of your brain that's associated with attention and focus. What this means is when you're practicing being more mindful this can help us notice when we're spacing out and then it causes us to refocus our attention to what our partner is telling us. This also lets us zone in on what our partner is needing or what they might be feeling. What this does is help us create a more loving relationship, and it helps us build intimacy, both emotional and mental.

This is turn causes our relationship to be happier and more connected. Mindfulness is also great because it improves the emotion regulation that happens in our bodies when you're practicing mindfulness. It improves the connectivity between certain areas of your brain, and it'll send a message to your brain to stop certain responses. It will have you relax, so this means that when we lose our temper instead of getting upset about it or running away, we will stop ourselves from doing that before we have upset our partners.

When we practice being mindful, it also helps us with our self-awareness. Practicing being mindful on a day to day basis leads to changes in our brain like the other aspects are being mindful. The difference is that this part of being mindful actually helps us observe when we're acting out in unhealthy ways. Mindfulness can help us when we get angry, but another benefit is it helps us redirect our attention back to how we would like to be acting, what we stand for, and what our values are.

Another thing that this does for us is that it helps us restrain the impulse to act out destructively, and it helps us restrain the impulse of wanting to manipulate our partners. No one should ever manipulate their partner in any way, and you should never hurt them on purpose. Anything we can do to restrain that impulse is important. It helps even to do something else when you're tempted to hurt your partner. Along with practicing mindfulness if you find that you and your partner are genuinely hurting each other, you should seek help right away.

Mindfulness studies have also shown that when we practice mindfulness, our emotions change as well. Instead of automatically shutting down emotionally or starting to attack your partner with angry words, we start becoming more mindful, and as such, we have less desire to be in what is known as threat mode. What this does for couples is it can get them out of a destructive cycle, and it can help them out of negativity along with it. This is especially important because it also helps with emotional distance. Couples want to embrace emotional intimacy with each other, and many find that they can have issues with it. As such, this will help couples communicate better while strengthening their emotional bond.

Perhaps the most important part of acting mindfully is that it makes us more empathetic people. Empathy is important to help couples be able to communicate freely with each other, and it can help couple's feel closer to each other as well. Another benefit of being more empathetic is that it helps us learn how to approach our partner compassionately, and it helps us stay away from the anger impulse. This can take the conversation in a completely different direction which can be a great thing for couples. Compassion helps us express warmth to our partner and love to them.

Love and warmth are also a big part of building intimacy. Mindfulness creates this approach and helps us become more loving instead of being in a mindset of avoidance. It helps us to keep away from not wanting to talk to our partners as well since it helps open us up to communication. When we begin to be mindful and make sure that we are practicing mindfulness on a daily basis we can reap the benefits of mindfulness not only helping us become more empathetic but helping us become better in our relationships.

Another benefit of being mindful and practicing it on a daily basis is that you get to make sure that you're staying on top of your empathetic abilities and to make sure that your keeping yourself attuned to them. We can also make sure that we are staying in that loving headspace.

If you feel stressed and need a breather to calm yourself or when we need to stop what we're doing we can try a breathing technique that can help you calm down when we're feeling upset or stressed. One breathing technique that can really help is called the 5 to 7. The 5 to 7 is where you breathe in for a count of 5 and then release for a count of 7. This helps to destress you and helps you relax, making sure that you're calm. This is going to help you in turn not be so stressed out with your partner because you're in a calm headspace yourself.

Another thing about mindfulness that's important for us to understand is that it helps us get to a place of understanding. It also helps us come to the understanding things that we shouldn't be doing in a relationship and things that we should. There are ways that we shouldn't be treating our partner and the ways that we should.

When you want communication in your relationship, and you want to make sure that the relationship doesn't break down, you should remember that by being mindful of yourself and mindful of your partner is going to help you see how the two of you can act together when you're not in a place of anger and mistrust.

Another plus to being mindful is that it will serve to help your relationship become much more stable along with helping your emotional connection and your bond as a couple. Your bond as a couple needs to remain unified instead of tearing apart. This is why these tips are great for helping people understand what they should be paying attention to in a relationship and for themselves.

Our partners need to be mindful of us as we should be paying attention to them and there are many different ways that we can help our communication skills and strengthen the bonds of love and relationship that we share with our mate. By strengthening the bonds of love, you are helping your bonds become whole again even if they have been fractured or damaged. By practicing mindful relationship tips and skills on a day to day basis with yourself you will be able to understand yourself better and know what you need to do to improve for your own happiness and the same can be said for your partner when you begin to become more mindful of everything that's going on around you.

Mindfulness helps us when we are zoning out and paying attention to the things that don't matter as well. Everyone has so much going on in their heads on a daily basis that if we just tune in to what's going on in our lives and tune the other things out, we can experience new benefits in our lives. Then we are more able to pay attention to the people in our life that do matter.

The same can be said about work. When you use the tips that you have learned about mindfulness in your everyday life, you will be able to be more attentive at work as well, and you will be able to focus yourself and drive yourself more in your professional life as well. This is a great thing because your personal life improves, but then your work and professional life do as well. It's a great thing when we improve all aspects of our life and not just one.

CHAPTER 7: IDENTIFYING SIGNS OF TROUBLE

Defining narcissist

This chapter is concerned with defining and describing the narcissist personality, identifying its origins and the characteristics and qualities that one may use to identify this trait in oneself or in another person. It also describes how individuals gradually turn narcissist in adulthood, and also how some people acquire the traits from not changing their personalities and emotional issues from childhood. The origin of the condition in a person's childhood will also be discussed, including the pathological capacity of this personality disorder.

1.0: Definition of a narcissist

The narcissist is a character trait whereby an individual is overly obsessed with their own self, expecting unconditional regard and adoration and being mindless of the effects of their nature toward other people. Narcissism is a personality disorder of the excessive and exaggerated sense of importance above all others. A narcissist is a self-centered individual who expects to acquire automatic recognition and compliance from their environment.

This person also bears natural selfishness which entails an uncontrollable desire to own or to be in charge of most of the best resources in any association. Whether competing in uniqueness or cost-wise, the narcissist wants to feel that they own the best items. They also want to believe they are the best in any recognizable argument or debate, and that they have the ideal opinions and ideologies in any arena. The narcissist character also doesn't function in any environment in which they do not feel specially treated and regarded. They have an unnatural desire for the feeling of uniqueness and believing that they are greater, or should be greater than any other people.

Their mentalities are more oriented toward a hierarchical social setting where everyone has a particular rank or caliber, against the communal society which embraces equality, with the expectation that the top positions belong to them. These people also bear a built-in personality that is so difficult to be close to. They have exaggerated self-love, which makes them appear mean and boastful and proud. Narcissist personality also characterizes an exaggerated and distorted sense of reality.

Their perceptions and beliefs about love, work, achievement, abilities, and life, in general, are unusually inflated and non-factual. They tend to be highly imaginative and regard their abilities as superior, sometimes too much to be possible. They like to express their prowess in an unreal manner and give exaggerated views about life, or regarding their past achievement. This exaggeration is also reflected in their physical appearances.

Narcissists are excessively obsessed with their physiques as they believe that they are the best, be it best looking, best dressed, most beautiful or handsome, and that any flaw in their appearance is not tolerated or acceptable to them. They will be seen to spend hefty amounts of time and resources in a bid to look the best, eliminating any competition in regard to fashion and looks. Any external party that proves competitive and threatens their appearance or their social status is considered intrusive and something that should be dealt with. Not only do these narcissist characters want to feel superior and important, but they also expect that special recognition from the people around them, and also have that sense of entitlement, either in being awarded the best resource or in commanding ultimate submission from the people in their environment.

The narcissist is also associated with another quality that might be of great advantage in some situations in life. The fact that they believe to be better than other people indicates a positive attitude that puts them at the top positions, whether in management, competitive activities, or leadership. This kind of character is uncomfortable in any situation that doesn't put him/heart the top position. This means that they will do all in their abilities to make sure they retain the best positions or items in society, even when it entails disregarding other people's rights or needs in order to get there. This success-oriented nature may be helpful in getting through some situations in life; however, it is mostly only beneficial to the person, and mostly ends up hurting or inconveniencing other people in the process.

A narcissist is thus hard to get along with, who desires unquestionable and insatiable compliance and regard from other people, whilst bearing no empathy to other people.

1.1: Narcissism in history

The narcissist concept has been in existence since the first century AD. Some myths have been recorded and interpreted as to highlight the basic characteristics of narcissism and the main orientations of narcissistic personalities. One myth is about a man who got reprimanded for his personal conviction that he had a more brilliant mind than that of the god Zeus. His punishment was to push a stone up, then down a mountain every day. The object of the punishment according to the narrator, Sisyphus, was due to a depiction of grandiosity and extreme supremacy on this man that resulted to the treasonable act, which is a key feature of a narcissistic personality.

Another myth from the Greek chapters, as recorded by the Romans a couple of thousand years ago, gives a more detailed account on the subject, and is also the origin of the term 'narcissism.' A renowned Roman psychologist and poet known as Ovid coined this story of Narcissus, which is the name of the subject of the myth and also of a brilliant white flower that was named after the myth.

The story describes Narcissus as an admirable, attractive and extremely self-loving and proud youth, wreaking youthful beauty and charm, but the whose obsession to his own self made him very scared and incapable of loving or accepting love from any other person who adored him. Just in the peak of his adolescence, Narcissus one day went deep into the woods where he encountered a young girl called Echo, who was obsessed with him and kept making advances, all of which Narcissus avoided or fled from. This incident was among many other attempts by interested suitors to have Narcissus's attention in vain. Narcissus's mother was compelled to seek therapeutic assistance for her son, where he learned that Narcissus would not succeed in his life unless he discovered himself.

Many attempts from suitors eventually caused bitterness and resentment in these suitors to a point where one of them, in vengeance, sought the intervention of the goddess Nemesis, in a bid to make Narcissus feel love but be denied of possessing the thing he loves most. With the wish granted, Narcissus was directed to a pool where he was awed and deeply encapsulated by his magnificent image in the mirrored reflection on the pool.

This image captured his attention so long that he couldn't move away from the sight, and thus he eventually wasted and grew into the Narcissus flower, giving rise to the concept of narcissism.

These myths all highlight the very basic principles of a narcissistic personality. It is observable that the main quality of the main character in both Sisyphus's and Ovid's narratives is grandiosity. The Narcissus's tale also depicts the inability to love another person, the absence of empathy in a person's actions and the uncontrollable urge for mirroring. These are the four major schools of a narcissist and are the chief characteristic qualities of the early, infantile stages of life, which everyone should once bear.

During this early stage of human development, the individuals are almost entirely dependent and entitled to unconditional attention, causing them to perceive everyone or every process on their environments as a part of themselves, or as a continuation of their own selves. In the cases where an individual is unwilling or is unable to progress from this mentality and lets the attitude to progress to adulthood, this is where the condition is described as a personality disorder that should be addressed.

In the early 20th century, other psychoanalysts such as Otto Kernberg and Sigmund Freud were among the first people who modified and advanced the theory of narcissism and its new developments and effects in society through further research and social study. In 1911, Kernberg was the first to attempt to relate excessive self-admiration to narcissism. He later described three principal forms of a narcissistic personality, infantile, adult and pathological narcissism, the first two which are acceptable, and the third characterizing a social and personal disorder which requires attention and correction.

In 1914, Freud also made more progress in the understanding of narcissism, where he related the narcissistic nature to the manner and direction to which a person's libido is focused. He explained that an individual's drive toward one's survival instincts could be manifested toward oneself or toward another party or object.

During the development of one's personality and identity from childhood, a person's relationship and interaction with the immediate environment can either cause the person to build uncontrollable self-love or to translate their love toward another person or thing. Transferring one's love to another party depletes the person's primal narcissism or self-love, leaving them very vulnerable to emotional and physical abuse due to the inability to take care of oneself, leading to a dependent personality, while the excessive self-love leads to the extension of the primal narcissism into adulthood, resulting to narcissistic personality disorder.

Later in the century, Heinz Kohut, in the 1970s, introduced three variations under the narcissistic personality; the mirroring character, the idealizing character, and the grandiose character. These variations created a better way of understanding and classifying narcissist personalities in society. These classes have progressively developed to create further sub-classes of a narcissist as observed in society such as the exhibitionist narcissist, the vulnerable narcissist, the malignant narcissist, the social and the anti-social narcissist. Christopher Lasch, in 1979, described the American population as being pathologically victimized by a narcissistic personality disorder, attributed to the broken social support system that had gradually developed in American society.

1.2: Narcissistic traits

In this section, we will make an exploration of the specific character traits that can be combined in an individual to warrant him or her as being a narcissist. These are all observable and experiential personal qualities that the narcissists possess and how they unknowingly express these characteristics in society.

It is also of paramount importance to keep in mind that in the individual sense, there exist two primary classes of narcissists, the pro-social narcissist, and the anti-social narcissist. These two characters differ by manner and degree of association with people. The pro-social narcissists thrive in an arena where they do many positive deeds in a bid to earn their recognition from society through appreciation, regard, and sense of gratitude that will result from the reactions of the people who will benefit from, or acknowledge their effort. These people can be described as social dependents as they rely on pleasing the society by investing in and giving back to society.

The anti-social narcissist, on the other hand, is the complete opposite of the pro-social. He is the self-centered, arrogant, and uncaring personality who can only satisfy his ego by exploiting, demeaning, bullying, or oppressing others in order to achieve their purpose of safeguarding their elevated self-esteem. The following sub-topics will describe the main observable qualities of a narcissist.

A natural sense of entitlement

The people who exhibit narcissism have an uncontrollable self-belief of deserving exceptional treatment and accord from other people around him. They expect unquestionable compliance with their needs and views and require everyone around them to be automatically submissive to their expectations. They believe that they are special and expect to be treated so. In situations where this feeling is not given to them, or whenever they fail to gain that recognition, these people perceive that as an ambush to their idealized status and can cause serious injury to their egos.

This quality may, however, be easily confused with the superiority entitlement that can be observed in leaders, employers, bosses, and prominent people. These classes have to behave in a superior manner and are treated especially courtesy of their social caliber. They may, however, be decent and normal people when outside their lines of administration. The true narcissistic personality disorder victim always wants special regard and treatment regardless of their status in society.

Arrogant behavior and lack of discretion

Another feature of a narcissistic personality disorder patient is open insensitivity to feelings, views, and needs of others around this person. In this way, they exhibit a bold arrogance which can be viewed in their manner of verbal communication, their gestures, and their reactions toward other people. They are never shy to openly express themselves to others and do not seem to be concerned about their feelings or emotions. This air-headed characteristic deems them as proud and pretentious persons and invokes fear, undeserved reverence, and feelings of hate and resentment towards this hateful personality.

Whether it is happening at home, at work, or during other peer associations, other people tend to avoid any debate or reference to any viewpoints that are associated with this character. The end effect is that these narcissists continue believing they are the most proficient in knowledge or achievement even when in the real sense, they have unreal and misguided perceptions regarding many aspects of life. As much as this attitude wins these individuals top positions in society, it also created a toxic quality of leadership that is more dictatorial and less rational. Chances of failure in these setups are high, and they always result with the narcissist translating all blame onto the other participants and events.

Disregard of personal boundaries and limits

Narcissism is also identifiable in those people who have no respect for social and personal boundaries. They are not able to differentiate between their ideologies and beliefs and as such they act in a manner to suggest that the views or beliefs of others are, or should be extensions of their own ideas. They do not respect the thin line between self and others. According to the narcissist, no one else is valid unless they are acting in this person's favor, or are providing narcissistic supply to this narcissist.

If you are not of any direct use to the narcissist, then you do not exist in his mind. They do not understand or are unwilling to acknowledge that everyone is equal by right and expression and that no one should be treated less or more favorably than the other. This narcissist will not respect or regard anyone who fails to be a participant in replenishing his narcissistic food. This narcissistic supply may be physical or emotional. It may be attention and praise, submission and adherence, recognition or adoration, or it may be in the form of material or substance supply. The narcissist will not mind about the feelings of anyone whose boundaries they have crossed, and may not even realize that they are making another person uncomfortable in the process. They can take from, or ambush another person and not show any remorse for their actions.

Lack of empathy toward other people

Individuals suffering from narcissistic personality disorders find it hard to love or care about other people's feelings and well-being in their environments. They have little or no interest at all in any normal, loving interpersonal attachments or associations with other people. This lack of empathy for others is fostered by a feeling of great emptiness and unworthiness, which this person with the disorder has learned to try to cover up with the coldness and lack of empathy by wanting to be acknowledged and treated as the best or the most valuable persons in society.

As such, this person is either unwilling or unable to recognize and respect the feelings and needs of those around him. They do not like to be associated with the weak, humble, caring, or affectionate people as they consider those as weaknesses that should not be tolerated. They instead like to dominate in the proud, pretentious, competitive, boastful, and ruthless environment, where competition for dominance and adoration is all that matters to one's ego.

Illusive and unrealistic thinking

Narcissists are observed to have an unreal and impractical way of perceiving various ideologies in life. They tend to believe that their thinking is perfect and often get caught up in unreal fantasies that are in view of the idealized perfect world that they feel belongs to them. These fantasies revolve around the best positions of power, the best potential partners, being the most brilliant in some aspect or another, and being the most successful or influential person in their social domains.

This magical thinking portrays the kind of lifestyle or social status that these narcissistic personality disorder victims expect to be living. These characters are also known to have a constant urge to exaggerate their accomplishments and abilities in order to appear superior and more worthy of special recognition to the other person. They may be observed to boast about past achievements that in the real sense weren't as successful, or never even existed in their lives, all in a bid to convince their audience into perceiving them and treating them as more special in society.

Exploiting others for the benefit of self

People with NPD are seen to be fond of using or misusing others in order to achieve their own inflated needs. They are not cautious of the other person's welfare or wishes as long as theirs is addressed first. This exploitation may be in the form of mental, material, or emotional abuse. In most cases, the person who is being exploited is hardly aware of the abuse as it is a well-orchestrated plan by the abuser. The victim of the abuse ends up wasting his/her mental, emotional, or material resources on this narcissist without any gain or gratitude. Once the relationship is over, the abuser does not even realize that he has injured someone for their benefit.

Uncontrolled envy and pretense

Narcissistic individuals have an acquired belief that other people are envious of them and their accomplishments. In this way, they also secretly and overly envy those people they consider as equal or superior to them in their idealized personalities. If a person believes that they are, or are bound to be the best in leadership or in material riches, he may be envious of an existing great leader or wealthy person. Since this feeling is in mind, envy will still prevail even if this narcissist is miles away from attaining that status which he is envious of.

There are many more characteristics that describe a person with a narcissistic personality disorder. They all seem to converge to a character who has an exaggerated sense of entitlement, validity, and self-importance with an inherent disregard for any external view or party that does not comply with the person's needs. There is, however, a healthy form of narcissism that should be in every person. The healthy form of self-worth is about loving oneself and taking care of oneself in all aspects of life. This is a natural mechanism that protects the person from illness and abuse. However, if this feeling of self-appreciation comes with disregard to other people's feelings and needs, then it is termed as harmful narcissism.

CHAPTER 8 HEALING

In this chapter, we will discuss the part that comes after conflict or self-conflict. The part that comes after you use nonviolent communication or violent communication. This part is healing. There are several ways that we will look at healing, involving both

yourself and others.

Healing involves several components, as it is a complex process. It involves reaching a solution to the satisfaction of everyone involved, using empathy to do so, and carrying this empathy on into every other part of your life.

HEALING AND RECONCILIATION WITHOUT COMPROMISE

One of the main things that sets nonviolent communication apart from other types of communication or communication styles is the way that it deals with conflict or problem solving. We touched on this earlier, but here we will examine it in more detail.

The way that nonviolent communication views conflict or problem solving involves reaching a solution that does not involve compromise. This type of problem solving involves a solution where both people are comfortable, and their needs are met. You may think that this is not possible, but that is likely because the type of communication that you are used to is the violent sort- especially in conflict resolution. This is of no fault of yours, it is how we are taught to communicate, and this process of learning to use nonviolent communication can be seen as an unlearning of violent communication.

The way that this works is that both people are expressing their needs or values, and this ensures that neither of them has to give up having their needs met. In a regular confrontation, nobody's needs are talked about. They are usually hidden. Because of this, nobody is aware of each other's needs and a compromise is the way that the conflict is resolved in order to reach a conclusion. The problem with compromise is that since nobody's values or needs are talked about, the compromise usually involves both people settling for something less-than-ideal. If you lay your needs out on the table, it is made known that any solution that takes your needs into consideration will be a welcome one.

To help you better understand this, I will explain the difference between a compromise and a NVC solution, or satisfaction. A compromise involves each person setting aside or giving up their need or their value in order to reach a solution. Satisfaction, on the other hand, involves each person's need being met. The difference seems simple, but it is much more complex in real-world situations, especially when everyone is used to having to give up their needs in a time of conflict. Normally, the compromise is the solution that is achieved with the least amount of effort, and this is the one that is most often opted for. It comes from the perspective of, "if I can't get my need met, than neither should you." This idea is not good for anyone, and it perpetuates negativity and self-centredness. The solution that involves satisfaction may take more dialogue and more work, but it is the best possible resolution.

USING NONVIOLENT COMMUNICATION TO REACH SATISFACTION

The way that this looks in practice is with each person using NVC to communicate their needs to the other.

1. Person 1 uses a NVC statement to express their feeling and need, ending with a request.
2. Person 2 does the same.
3. Ensure that both of you have understood each other's needs. If this is not the case, ask for clarification without judgment and continue to try to understand each other's needs.
4. Use empathy to understand the other person's feelings and needs. (We will look at this in more detail soon.)
5. If both of your requests do not work together, both of you can propose alternate options for resolution ensure to avoid demanding or judgmental language.

In order to know whether or not you understand the other person's needs, you can monitor their reaction to what you are saying. For example, if the person responds with something like "I don't want to talk about it." To this, you can respond with "Am I not understanding you properly?" If the person responds with yes or no answers, this signals to you that there is still something preventing them from being fully open with you. Maybe they are unaware of their emotions or their need. You can help them to come to this realization by guessing their need or feeling or asking them some more questions to help them open up. This involves some work, but it will lead to the best possible solution. Keep monitoring their answers and their behavior. If they begin to open themselves up in terms of body language or conversation, you are likely getting close to their need. Once you have found it, continue with the steps.

EMPATHY

I briefly mentioned empathy when discussing the steps to take in order to reach satisfaction when problem solving. Empathy is quite necessary when it comes to problem solving and conflict, as it enables you to reach a solution with compassion instead of anger. Before looking at empathy in a broader sense in terms of how it can serve us in our everyday lives, we are going to look at the different types of empathy that exist.

Affective

Empathy is the ability to share someone else's feelings. It is also the ability to understand the feelings of another. It also involves responding according to this shared emotion.

Somatic

The next type of empathy is called somatic empathy. This type of empathy involves a real, physical reaction to someone else's feelings. For example, if you see that your friend is embarrassed and your face starts to turn red out of second-hand embarrassment.

Cognitive

The third and final type of empathy is cognitive empathy. This type of empathy is when you are able to understand another person's feelings to the point of being able to understand their mental state when feeling that emotion and being able to imagine what they may be thinking or what their thought process may be.

The most common form of empathy, affective empathy (hereafter, empathy), is the ability of a person to share someone else's feelings. It is also the ability to understand the feelings of another. The difference between empathy and sympathy is that sympathy only involves feeling sorry for the feelings someone else is going through, whereas empathy involves putting yourself in their shoes in order to feel what they must be feeling.

Empathy is important in nonviolent communication and problem solving using nonviolent communication because of the way that it gets a person to understand the needs of the other and express genuine interest in helping them have their needs met. It due to this that nonviolent communication problem solving is effective- because each person is able to fully understand and connect with the need of the other and the feeling that having this need unmet causes.

To give you an idea of what sympathy versus empathy feels like, here is an example. If you have ever had someone open up to you about what they are feeling due to something terrible happen in their lives, did you pity them? Or did you put yourself in their shoes in order to really feel what this terrible event must be making them feel? The former would be sympathy. The latter would be empathy.

WHAT CAN EMPATHY DO?

Empathy, when brought into every aspect of a person's life can have powerful effects on their relationships and their life in a general sense. Empathy has the power to do all of the following and more,

Heal

Empathy has the power to heal. This is because, in order to heal, we need other people. In order to have other people remain there for us in the toughest of times, they need empathy. When they have empathy, they are able to understand what we are going through, what we may need and what they can do for us.

Empathy also helps to heal by bridging gaps through creating understanding. When there is a conflict of any sort, there needs to be healing after the conflict is resolved, especially if the conflict involved angry words or hurt feelings. After a conflict of this sort, empathy is required in order to bridge the gap between the parties involved. They must reach a mutual understanding in order to heal and empathy is what allows this to happen.

Strengthen

Empathy also has the power to strengthen. Empathy allows relationships to grow and promotes intimacy among people, even if only in a platonic way. By having empathy, it creates a closeness because of the understanding it brings about someone else. When you can understand another person, this strengthens your bond.

If you have a friend that you are extremely close with, think of what you would feel if they came to you crying. How would you feel if they told you that they were going through something tough. You would likely share their feelings with them even if you were not going through it yourself. This is empathy at work. This is the kind of thing that makes your bond so strong and that makes you feel so close to this person.

Imagine if this type of empathy existed among people who had had their differences. Or people who just met. Or two people who were arguing over a parking spot. This would strengthen their connection even if it was the first time that they had met.

Calm the Mind

Empathy is able to calm the mind. This is because it allows a person to practice gratitude and brings them into the present moment. Empathy and meditation are closely linked. Meditation brings about feelings of calm and awareness, while empathy does quite the same.

Break the Silence

Finally, empathy can break the silence. What this means is that it can lead to intimacy and connection, which also leads to dialogue among people. It is very difficult to be open and vulnerable with people, but if you know that you share mutual empathy, you know that they will understand that they will not judge you and that you can be safely open and vulnerable with them. This is helpful for people who have a hard time opening up and who don't readily speak their feelings or share their thoughts.

EMPATHY IN RELATIONSHIPS

There are many different types of relationships that a person has at one time in their life. Empathy in relationships is defined as understanding within the heart, which allows us to see the beauty in the other person. Empathy is beneficial in every type of relationship. Below are all of these different types of relationships ordered from most intimate to least intimate.

Romantic

Familial

Friend

Colleague

Teacher/ Education

Acquaintance

Unknown

These relationships are all different, but the thing that they all have in common is that they all involve empathy in order to make or keep them strong.

Romantic

It goes without saying that a romantic relationship will involve empathy. The two people involved in a romantic relationship are so closely linked on an emotional level that empathy is a given. If your romantic partner comes home after a bad day, you can likely feel their tiredness and their stress even if you had an alright day. This kind of connection between two people is built on intimacy and with that comes empathy. Since empathy in relationships is defined as understanding within the heart that allows us to see the beauty in the other person, this explains why in a romantic relationship you see beauty in the other person no matter what they are doing- even if they have just finished at the gym and are covered in sweat.

Using empathy in your communication with your partner shows them that you are listening to them, that you value their needs and that you understand their feelings. This promotes trust, feelings of security, and sensitivity. A healthy relationship is built on communication and this is why using empathetic communication is so important in a romantic relationship. To avoid resentments or miscommunications, it is necessary and important to express your needs in a clear way to your partner.

Familial

A familial relationship is not always intimate, but in many cases, it is the next most intimate after a romantic relationship. In a familial relationship, there is the ever-present fact that you have been with each other through everything and have grown up together, seeing each other in any and every situation that makes this so intimate. This relationship always involves empathy as a family is something that is forever, and always there for you.

This is why the ways that family members communicate with each other is so important, especially in front of children who are still learning, growing, and developing. The important thing to teach here is that empathy and compassion come before behavior management, even if there are feelings of frustration or disappointment present. It is okay to feel disappointed in someone or frustrated with their behavior, but it is important to show them that you are still empathetic and compassionate toward them regardless. This is a key difference between violent and nonviolent communication, where violent communication often involves the use of anger and raised voices in times of frustration.

The way that nonviolent communication views problem solving is also extremely important when it comes to familial relationships. By modeling for your family members that problem-solving and conflict resolution involves satisfaction for everyone, you are showing them that they do not have to give up their needs and values in order to reach a resolution. This is, of course, provided they are needs that are considered to be among the hierarchy of needs and not needs such as "I need that chocolate bar," but this is what can be taught when modeling this type of problem-solving.

Friend

In many cases, a close friendship is the next most intimate relationship after a romantic one, so familial and friend relationships can be interchangeable in terms of their positioning on this list. With a very close friendship, you will feel closely linked to that person in terms of your emotions, and you have likely gone through many of the same things at the same time. This leads to a mutual understanding and an ability to understand each other on a deep emotional level.

Colleague

A colleague relationship is not the most intimate of relationships, but it is one where empathy can still prove very helpful. In a colleague relationship, you often are required to complete tasks together, and there are many situations that could turn into some type of conflict since it involves a lot of time and stress. In many cases, your colleagues are people who you see every day, and this develops a closeness that is different from many other relationships. Even if you are not in the type of relationship with your colleagues that involves sharing your deepest fears and dreams, you can still share your needs and feelings with them in order to reach a mutual understanding involving empathy. This will lead to a better working relationship and a more comfortable work environment for you, where your needs are met, and you feel empathy from others.

Using nonviolent communication and empathy among colleagues will keep the workplace people-focused. Too often, workplaces become focused on numbers and results and rules and deadlines. By using nonviolent communication in the workplace, you are able to remind everyone that there are still human feelings and needs present behind all of the numbers and targets. Often, even the management within a workplace uses violent communication in order to try to motivate and push their staff members. This type of motivation is what we are so used to being exposed to. However, it leads to stressful work environments and competition among colleagues. This type of communication is not effective for long-term motivation as people eventually become resentful and tired of being seen as another producer.

Teacher/ Education

Education is a place where the forms of communication that are used are very important to the development of the people being taught. In schools for children, they learn much more than just how to count and how to write, they also learn necessary life skills and interpersonal skills. Part of this is learning how to communicate effectively. It is for this reason that using empathetic communication, or nonviolent communication in schools is so important. Nonviolent communication for kids allows them to learn in a judgment-free and shame-free environment, which is essential to their development as mentally healthy adults with a healthy level of self-esteem.

The way that kids are communicated to most often in the school system is by way of threatening the "bad" and rewarding the "good." This is one of the facets of violent communication, as it is a method of controlling outcomes in order to get what one wants out of people. By having this modeled for children, they learn that the way they can get what they want as an adult is through violent communication, including threats, rewards, and the absence of empathy or compassion.

By using empathy and nonviolent communication in the classroom, it promotes feelings of safety, trust, interpersonal bonds, collaboration, learning, and acceptance. This is the ideal environment that kids need to learn and grow to their full potential.

Acquaintance

With an acquaintance, you may not think that you would need to feel any empathy towards them. In many cases, however, your acquaintances are responsible for helping you with things or are people you pass on a daily basis, and exercising empathy here will be a nice thing for both of you. If you can understand them and they can understand you, there is one more person in the world who you can say you have a positive relationship with. That is a greatly positive thing.

Unknown

While this may seem like the last relationship in which empathy would be beneficial or required, it is actually quite helpful for you and the person who you don't know if you share mutual empathy. This is because this person may be someone who you pass on the street, someone who works at the coffee shop you went to or someone who is in the parking lot looking for a spot to park at the same time as you. In any of these cases, approaching the situation with empathy will help you to have these small interactions throughout your day without conflict or strife, but with understanding and a pleasant feeling.

SELF-EMPATHY

Another type of empathy is empathy with and for oneself. You are often the person you forget when talking about things like how you choose to speak to someone and the way in which you solve problems. We must not forget that you yourself are as much deserving of your love, kindness, and empathy as anyone else is. You are usually your own worst critic. The way that you assume everyone else is thinking about you is much harsher than any way anyone has ever thought about you other than yourself.

Self-empathy is defined as a compassionate, deep awareness of your own inner experience. This awareness of your inner experience must be met with empathy. You may be aware of your inner experience and approach it with judgmental and shame-filled thoughts and words. This is not practicing empathy.

Often times, the way that you talk to yourself is the way that you will talk to others. By changing the way that you talk to other people, you are also showing yourself that you should talk to yourself in this way, as well. By showing empathy to yourself in the same way that you do the most important people in your life, you are more likely to experience good mental health, a lower risk of depression, and a greater level of self-satisfaction. You are also better able to forgive yourself for things that you deem to be negative or bad decisions, which allows you to move forward without bringing with you all of the things you feel you have failed at.

EMPATHY IN NONVIOLENT COMMUNICATION

Nonviolent communication cannot be found without empathy. If there is no empathy, then you are not truly using nonviolent communication. In order to use nonviolent communication to resolve conflict or solve problems, all parties must use empathy in order to come to a solution where everyone is satisfied. Why you may ask? Because if there was no empathy in a situation like this, then every person involved would be wondering why they can't have it their way and why other people's needs are important. In the presence of empathy, these thoughts are not present. This is because empathy leads to the understanding of the needs of others and the understanding that everyone's needs are just as important as your own.

SELF-EMPATHY AND BODY IMAGE

Negative body image usually comes about from years of hearing negative comments from others, which we internalize over time. This leads us to believe these negative things about ourselves, and negative body image or self-image, in general, is the result. Another way that we may develop negative body image is by constantly comparing ourselves to other people in real life, on television and on social media. Self-empathy and nonviolent communication help to improve body image. This is for many reasons. I have outlined these reasons below.

Firstly, it allows you to get in touch with your deeper feelings and connect them to your needs, which, in turn, encourages you to do healthy self-exploration. By noticing your feelings and your needs that cause these feelings to arise, you can see that there is nothing inherently wrong with you and that you are simply a human being who is motivated by basic human needs. This helps to put things into perspective and shows you that you are just like everyone else.

Next, self-empathy and nonviolent communication help to improve body image by modeling the ways that you should be speaking to others, which shows you the way that you should be speaking or thinking to yourself as well. By learning the differences between violent and nonviolent communication and beginning to use NVC in your life, it helps bring to your awareness the number of times that you have been using violent communication when talking to yourself. This awareness will help you change the way you talk to yourself by removing blaming, shaming and judging and replacing it with self-empathy.

By using nonviolent communication in your interactions, this shows other people how to use it in response. When other people use it in response to you, you are able to feel what it is like to be on the receiving end of empathy, and this can highlight for you why it is so important to do this to yourself.

You may think, "if it is this nice to feel empathy once, imagine how it would be to feel it every time I speak to myself."

There are specific times where your body image or your self-image is the lowest. This may happen on beach vacations or on holidays. By recognizing this, you can intervene in your regular thought processes and use self-empathy and nonviolent communication to combat this.

Finally, the ways in which self-empathy and NVC can help you to develop a greater level of self-image is when you use it to resolve problems or conflicts. By using NVC to resolve conflicts or solve problems with others, this showcases to yourself that you are capable of using NVC effectively and that you are capable of remedying situations without the use if violent communication. This is just as true when solving problems within your own mind. By voicing your needs to others and reaching a solution that does not require you to compromise, you are able to show yourself that you can do this any time for any situation, especially those within yourself. This will lead to a higher level of self-confidence and self-esteem, which are greatly beneficial for improving self-image.

SELF-EMPATHY AND BODY IMAGE

Negative body image usually comes about from years of hearing negative comments from others, which we internalize over time. This leads us to believe these negative things about ourselves and negative body image or self-image, in general, is the result. Another way that we may develop negative body image is by constantly comparing ourselves to other people in real life, on television, and on social media. Self-empathy and nonviolent communication help to improve body image. This is for many reasons. I have outlined these reasons below.

Firstly, it allows you to get in touch with your deeper feelings and connect them to your needs, which, in turn, encourages you to do healthy self-exploration. By noticing your feelings and your needs that cause these feelings to arise, you can see that there is nothing inherently wrong with you and that you are simply a human being who is motivated by basic human needs. This helps to put things into perspective and shows you that you are just like everyone else.

Next, self-empathy and nonviolent communication help to improve body image by modeling the ways that you should be speaking to others, which shows you the way that you should be speaking or thinking to yourself as well. By learning the differences between violent and nonviolent communication and beginning to use NVC in your life, it helps bring to your awareness the number of times that you have been using violent communication when talking to yourself. This awareness will help you change the way you talk to yourself by removing blaming, shaming, and judging and replacing it with self-empathy.

By using nonviolent communication in your interactions, this shows other people how to use it in response. When other people use it in response to you, you are able to feel what it is like to be on the receiving end of empathy, and this can highlight for you why it is so important to do this to yourself.

You may think, "if it is this nice to feel empathy once, imagine how it would be to feel it every time I speak to myself."

There are specific times where your body image or your self-image is the lowest. This may happen on beach vacations or on holidays. By recognizing this, you can intervene in your regular thought processes and use self-empathy and nonviolent communication to combat this.

Finally, the ways in which self-empathy and NVC can help you to develop a greater level of self-image is when you use it to resolve problems or conflicts. By using NVC to resolve conflicts or solve problems with others, this showcases to yourself that you are capable of using NVC effectively and that you are capable of remedying situations without the use if violent communication. This is just as true when solving problems within your own mind. By voicing your needs to others and reaching a solution that does not require you to compromise, you are able to show yourself that you can do this any time for any situation, especially those within yourself. This will lead to a higher level of self-confidence and self-esteem, which are greatly beneficial for improving self-image.

COMPASSION

All of our discussion of empathy leads us to compassion. Compassion is considered to be a "higher-level emotion" meaning that it requires a person to be wise and more emotionally mature in order to experience it. Compassion is a form of empathy, meaning that it is a very similar emotion. The difference is that compassion is empathy without the feeling of being overtaken or overwhelmed by another person's feelings. This means that it is the feeling of empathy but a more refined form. The benefit of this is that compassion is an emotion that a person can always feel- in every interaction and with every person, whereas empathy can become overwhelming and exhausting if it is felt in every interaction that you have.

If you were reading along in the section about different relationships and wondering how you are going to remain empathetic in every interaction you have with every person. This section holds the answer to your question. Empathy can become very exhausting emotionally if you are always trying to put yourself into other people's shoes and fabricate the emotions that they are feeling in order to develop a deep understanding of them and what they are going through. Think back on the example that I described when your romantic partner comes home from a hard day at work, and you feel their stress and their fatigue even if your day was fine. This can become quite draining for you if you are always having an okay day, and your partner is going through a hard time at work. It is not realistic to think that every day, your mood will gravely decline every time you see your partner after work. This could lead you to eventually feel depressed and resentful. Further, you may wonder why it is not your okay mood that it picked up by your partner instead. This is where compassion becomes the answer. By having compassion for your partner, you are able to understand deeply that they had a bad day and that they have had many bad days lately, but this does not make your mood decline instantly. Knowing this about your partner, you can exercise compassion by bringing them a cup of tea and sitting with them after putting on their favorite show, or making them a nice dinner to cheer them up. In this way, you are aware of their feelings and can understand them, but this does not make you feel the exact same way as your partner.

This is a more mature form of understanding that comes with time and sometimes with age. This is especially relevant for people who tend to automatically be empathetic toward everyone and everything. Changing their empathy into compassion is the key to ensuring that you remain to understand without sacrificing your own mental health in the process.

HONEST SELF-EXPRESSION

Honest self-expression is what comes as a result of practicing nonviolent communication. Honest self-expression is defined as expressing oneself authentically in a way that is likely to inspire compassion in others. This is essentially what steps two and three in nonviolent communication entail. Expressing your true feelings and ensuring that the feelings you are expressing are the deepest ones you could find is quite intimidating and can make you feel extremely vulnerable. Connecting this deep feeling to a need is also another stage of vulnerability. Sharing your needs and values is likely not something that you do often. By sharing these things together at one time is sure to make you feel very vulnerable. These two things are both ways of expressing yourself authentically. Therefore, you are practicing honest self-expression. By deciding to be vulnerable even though it is hard and uncomfortable at times, this inspires compassion in others for a few reasons.

The first reason is that they can see you deciding to be vulnerable and open with them about your feelings. Everyone can relate to how difficult this is, and this makes them feel empathy or compassion for you in this situation. Second, because you are expressing a need and they know that this is a difficult thing to do, they will also feel empathy or compassion for this need, as being vulnerable shows them that this is important to you.

Empathetic and nonviolent communication comes down to recognizing and acknowledging common humanity among yourself and others.

CONCLUSION

In any relationship, communication is a vital part of keeping it as strong as it can be. Effective communication is what you need to be sure that it's going to last the test of time. This book has given you helpful hints and tips on how you can help your relationship survive the test of time and make sure that the two of you have a unified relationship and a unified bond with each other. There are some relationships that have difficulty standing the long run, and that's because they have communication issues, or their relationship has broken down because they're unable to talk to each other the way the that they need to talk to each other.

Another problem in the relationship is that you don't listen to the way you need to listen to your partner. Everyone needs to be heard, and everyone needs to know that their partners are with them for the long haul and that they understand who their partner is and what they stand for. Everyone needs to know that they're being appreciated for who they are inside and that the communication issues in a relationship can be fixed. This is what gives a relationship hope. You should never lose hope or faith in yourself, your partner, or your own faith. Keeping hope and faith in your relationship is vital because once you lose hope, you will see that your relationship isn't just floundering, it could be at the point of breaking.

In this book, we have taught you the benefits of not only listening emphatically but speaking in the same way. There are different ways to listen to people, and one of them is that you just listen. However, when you just listen, you could be missing the point of the conversation, or you could forget the conversation 10 minutes later because you weren't solidly invested in the conversation in the first place. This book teaches you how to avoid that and why empathetic listening is more important. When you begin to listen in this way, it lets you understand how your partner is feeling and puts you on their side of the story. In addition to this, it lets you walk in their shoes so that you can understand what it is that they are experiencing on their side of the story. You will be better equipped to deal with this issue and how you can fix the problem before it escalates into something that can't be fixed.

Along with the ability to listen in a new way, we offer to teach you how to speak correctly with your partner. When you are able to speak with an emphatic heart and use emphatic words, you are beginning to understand the impact your words can have on your partner and yourself. There are different ways that you can speak to your partner. There are also ways that you shouldn't speak to them. For example, you can speak to them rudely and uncaringly, or you could take the time and speak to them with loving words and respectful words. When you speak to your partner with respect and love instead of breaking them down with your words you're showing them that you're actually taking the time to understand what the conversation is about and that you want them to know you love them.

- It shows them that you're actually trying to fix what's wrong with them and that you're showing them that you take the time to listen to what they're saying. One thing that is so important is that when your speaking to them, you think before you speak. Speaking respectfully toward your partner helps them understand that you care about them and about how they feel. You're not trying to hurt them, and you're not trying to make the situation worse. What you're trying to do is communicate with your partner effectively so that problems like this don't occur in the future.

Compromise is a big part of a relationship as well, and we help you understand that you shouldn't manipulate your partner into getting what you want. What you should do instead is have an open and honest dialog. You should also be able to speak to them without manipulating them in order to get your way. On the other side of that, we also show you that compromise doesn't mean that that you lose your voice and that you lose who you are. We emphasize that you should be able to be who you are in your relationship and that you should not lose yourself. We help you understand how you can maintain being yourself in your relationship while making sure you are not losing yourself. We also teach you and give you helpful hints and tips about why you should accept your partner for who they are and why it's important to make sure that you appreciate them for who they are.

No relationship can work if you or your partner are hiding who you are, and you feel like you can't be who you truly are with your partner. Both of you need to be able to be exactly who you are without fear of being judged for it. Practicing a mindful relationship every day and making sure that your understanding the importance of having a mindful relationship with your partner is one of the most important things that this book can teach you. It is one of the most important lessons that this book has to offer because when you have a mindful relationship and you're actively searching to make your relationship better; this is what's going to make the difference between a relationship lasting a year and a relationship lasting a lifetime. When you understand that concept, you will become stronger over time, and practicing something every day makes it easier to do this. After it becomes easier, you can start seeing real changes in your relationship. You will begin to see positive changes in your relationship because of the work your putting into it. Effective communication becomes easier as well because you're making an effort and you're putting yourself in the mindset of knowing that something needs to be changed.

No relationship is perfect, and if you're not willing to put in the work when times get hard, you will notice that your relationship is faltering. With this book, you should be able to begin to take steps to communicate effectively. As such, your relationship will be able to gain strength and unity as the two of you become closer and more loving to each other.

Dear Reader

I am an emerging writer and, with the sales made from the book, I can continue my studies to publish other books on the subject. I would appreciate an honest review from you.

Thanks for your support

EFFECTIVE COMMUNICATION SKILLS

****

A PRACTICAL GUIDE THAT DEVELOPS AND IMPROVES YOUR WAY OF SPEAKING EFFECTIVELY IN RELATIONSHIPS: IN WORK, IN THE FAMILY AND IN THE LIFE OF A COUPLE

****

By Michael Cooper

INTRODUCTION

Human beings are supreme beings, because not only are they intelligent, they can also organize and overcome any obstacle that comes their way. However, human beings are not mind readers and need to be communicated to, so that they can understand each other. Poor communication is the number one cause of broken relationships- whether at work, family or other partnerships. Communication is a skill that has to be practiced so that one can be able to function fully as a social being. People with poor communication skills often end up feeling left out, or lonely, because they cannot pass their messages across effectively.

Communication can either be verbal or nonverbal. Of the two, the nonverbal method is the most effective method of communication because it enables one to understand what is not being said, and the emotions behind the message being passed. Thus, during the communication process, nonverbal communication should be paid attention to, because it informs one what to respond when to react, and how to respond. It also improved relationships, as messages will be passed and received effectively, which prevents conflict and misunderstanding.

Effective communication can be impeded by distractions, poor listening skills, low emotional intelligence levels, inability to read body language, and low empathy levels. Conversations should not be monologues, which means that all parties involved should actively take part. The listener should actively listen, while the speaker should be adept in passing the information. Personal biases should be put aside during the communication process to ensure that the message is perceived as intended.

When listening, people often:

Pretend to listen by nodding their heads actively.

Pick out pieces of information to respond to

Concentrate all their energy into the conversation, though this happens on very few occasions.

After listening, people often do the following.

Evaluate to assess whether they agree with the information given, or they do agree with it.

Examine by asking questions from their point of view, according to their biases and experiences.

Advice from their experiences or other people's lessons.

Interpret according to what they perceive.

It is paramount for people to understand that communication is a two-way street, and to fulfill the second part, one has to receive the message. Failure to correctly receive the message impedes the whole communication process and renders the conversation useless. Thus, listening is the first part of the communication process and should be done actively. Attention should be paid during the listening process so that one can pay attention to other components, such as body language and emotions.

Response to the information given should be made appropriately, and this is where empathy comes in. Compassion should be practiced when listening and during the response stage. It means that one should be able to walk a mile in the other person's shoes and perceive what they are trying to say. During the whole process, clarification should be sought after, so that the message is received well.

CHAPTER 1: BARRIERS TO COMMUNICATION

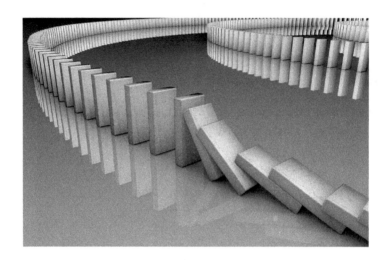

LINGUISTIC BARRIERS

Language is the principal tool used in communication, to mean that if parties want to communicate using different languages, then it becomes a barrier. Every major region in the world uses a specific vocabulary, which means that people from different areas cannot effectively communicate. Furthermore, a thick dialect can hinder effective communication, as a person may not understand the message being passed along. Research indicates that the dialect of each region changes every few kilometers, and that affects communication.

PSYCHOLOGICAL BARRIERS

Some mental conditions might affect effective communication. Some people have cognitive states, such as Wernicke's syndrome, which affects their ability to communicate effectively. Some have a phobia of speaking to crowds, speech disorders, or depression, which can hinder their ability to pass a message across effectively. Conditions like depression, social anxiety, and phobia can be treated, and the person can communicate effectively. However, those born with speech disorders might not have a treatment option. If they do, it will take time, thus affecting their ability to communicate effectively. Low self-esteem is another psychological disorder that can make people not to communicate effectively. Such people fear speaking out, for fear of being judged or ridiculed.

EMOTIONAL BARRIERS

A person's emotional intelligence will determine the ease by which he can communicate with his peers. A person with low emotional intelligence will not be at ease to pass his message along. However, a person with high emotional intelligence will communicate easily. A person who lets emotions take over when talking will not be able to communicate effectively. A perfect mix of emotions is needed to pass a message along effectively. Thus, a person is supposed to be able to identify their feelings, process them correctly, and display them in their message, in a way that does not impede the decision-making process.

PHYSICAL BARRIERS

It is the most known type of barrier, and once it is removed, effective communication can occur. It includes noise, faulty devices, walls, distance, and wind. Physical barriers make it hard for the message to be heard or seen by the receiver of the message. Thus, the message can be misconstrued or not be delivered at all. The only way to deal with physical barriers is to remove the source; for instance, the source of noise can be turned off, or the people communicating can move to a quiet place. An ample space can be a physical barrier, because sound might not be able to travel from one end of a room to the next, making communication hard.

CULTURAL BARRIERS

Different people from different parts of the world have their customs and rules that govern the use of language. Thus, some topics might be taboo, and such people might find it hard to express their emotions and use some words. Topics that are sensitive to discuss across cultures include politics, religion, race, disabilities, immigration, and sexuality. Thus, proper communication might not occur due to the differences and the volatile nature of such topics.

ORGANIZATIONAL BARRIERS

There are two types of communication in an organization; top-down and horizontal discussion. Depending on the type of disclosure an organization employs, there might be barriers to the way messages are passed, because some people might be privy to some information, while others are not. It will also depend on the level of authority a person has, and that can impede communication, especially for people low in the employment or social ladder.

ATTITUDE BARRIERS

Some people do not like interacting with people often. On the other hand, some people are incredibly social. Either way, it can be a hindrance to proper communication. Introverts might miss out on some information they would have acquired had they been more social. Extroverts might get the wrong message, or an overload of messages, due to their outgoing nature.

Some folk also have an attitude issue, which means that they have big egos and poor social behaviors. Thus, many people do not like interacting with them. Therefore, they might miss out on important information or misconstrue a message to fit their agenda or interests.

PERCEPTION BARRIERS

Perception is how a person perceives a message, and it has to be considered during the communication process. Different people can understand the same word differently, and that can impede communication because the message will not serve its intended purpose. It is how rumors start, and some rumors can be dangerous. A person who aims to pass a message should be aware of the perceptive level of the audience and use it to communicate effectively. The message should be precise and clear. Ambiguity should be avoided at all costs, to prevent different perceptions of the message.

PHYSIOLOGICAL BARRIERS

Some medical conditions or poor body functions can affect effective communication. Examples include dyslexia, stammering disorder, numbness, and deafness. They can all affect communication, especially in instances where specialists are not present to interpret their messages or interpret messages from the general public for them. The good thing is that these conditions can be treated, and with enough training, physiological barriers can cease to be a hindrance to effective communication.

TECHNOLOGICAL BARRIERS

The dynamic pace at which technology is developing makes it hard for everyone to keep up with new developments. Thus, it can at times become a barrier, especially for low-income areas, and areas with low network coverage. The invention of the internet also led to the design of internet slang, which may be hard to keep up with. this is due to the fast pace at which technology is moving.

Many people or organizations might not be able to purchase the latest gadgets for communication. Thus, it becomes a hindrance, as they will not be able to communicate effectively with people who have the latest gadgets. It is the reason why militaries opt for the newest technology so that they can have an advantage in communication over other armies.

PREJUDICES

Stereotypes might be good or bad, and they definitely affect communication. Due to a specific stereotype, a person will hear and perceive what they want to, rather than the real message. For instance, there have been complaints from women of the African American community that they are viewed as aggressive when they try to pass their point across. This stems from the stereotype that African American females are aggressive. As illustrated, prejudices can deny a specific group of people from being heard and this impeded communication. Prejudices also exalt some groups of people, and as a result, they are listened to more.

LACK OF ATTENTION, DISTRACTIONS, AND INAPPROPRIATENESS OF MESSAGE

Poor listening skills will affect communication because the message will not be adequately received. A message needs to be paid attention to so that the receiver can reply accordingly.

Distractions such as cellphones, technology, and noise can all affect communication. They change the attention of a person who in turn will not receive the message well.

If the message is irrelevant to the listener, it is unlikely that he will pay attention to it. Thus, it is paramount for a person to pass on the relevant message for it to be received well.

USE OF COMPLICATED WORDS

The use of jargon or technical terms for an audience that is not advanced will impede communication because they will not understand the message. People need to assess the education level of the audience before using complicated words.

The message will also turn to be irrelevant to the audience, even if it was meant for them. A speaker is to use words that can be understood easily, by everyone intended to receive the message. Thus, if fifty people can understand medical terms, and one person cannot, that one person should be considered so that everyone realizes the message.

MARITAL BARRIERS

When a couple finally ties the knot, it is paramount that their communication changes, because it is one of the most critical parts of a marriage. Between couples, there are psychological barriers, such as fear, insecurity, and unnecessary information that can impede proper communication. It is often the reason why couples say they are tired of each other after a while, and more often than not, it usually ends in divorce. Marriage can also be a barrier of communication, especially if the partners come from different backgrounds, and each fears voicing concerns for fear of offending the other.

COMMUNICATION FLOW

The communication flow theory states that people can communicate up to a certain level because the information they have is limited. Thus, more knowledgeable people have more things to talk about, and the conversation will take longer. Additionally, people who are more social hold more information because they have social means, and can hold a conversation for longer. Communication will be affected if a person's knowledge is limited, or is not very communicative, because the flow will be affected.

INAPPROPRIATE PRIORITIES

During communication, the priority is to pass a message or receive a message. However, these priorities might not be shared by both parties, or they might change in the course of communication for either of the parties. For instance, a group might want to discuss issues affecting teenage girls in an area, but a member of the group might feel like the conversation is a direct attack on men who engage adolescent girls. Thus, the discussion will not go on as planned, as one party will make it lag, or not happen at all. Misplaced priorities also mean that some people might not be on time to the venue so that effective communication can occur.

TUNNEL VISION

Tunnel vision means that an object cannot be depicted at 100% accurateness. In a conversation, tunnel-vision occurs when that situation is not clear, or the information given is not accurate. Thus, the receiver of the message cannot make a proper judgment because the accuracy is not at 100%. It mostly occurs when someone is at crossroads and wants to explain their side of the story. They mostly leave out the part where they were wrong, and this leads to tunnel vision for the receiver of the message.

TASK PREOCCUPATION

Communication with one party has to be done to completion before it can be taken up with someone else. Thus, when one is preoccupied with another task while communicating, it will not be clear. For instance, if a person is talking to a client about a product, then another client comes in and has to be informed about another product. If there is a shortage of time, both clients will not be communicated to effectively about the products, because the person passing the message will be preoccupied.

ACADEMIC CULTURE

Just like other cultures, each educational institution has a culture it adheres to. Each institution has different departments that have heads who lead the students. A professor might take a class where students might have differing opinions, and that might affect the educator's ability to drive his point home. Alternatively, a school has different cultures, religions, races. In the course of learning, they will develop a mutual culture that will promote learning. However, differences are bound to occur from time to time, and that will affect communication, and by extension, the learning process.

Some students might also find some units hard to decipher, and this will be a communication challenge, because of their inability to understand the information given from a logicl point of view.

LACK OF CONFIDENCE

Parties involved in a communication process must all possess the courage to hold it, regardless of whether it is oral or virtual. A person who does not have the confidence will not get his points across, and that will affect his ability to communicate effectively. Factors such as anxiety, nervousness all impede proper communication. Lack of confidence is only not noted in conversations, it will also be present in written conversations, and that affects communication.

CHAPTER 2: THE ART OF LISTENING IN COMMUNICATION

"We were given two ears but only one mouth, because listening is twice as hard as talking." - - Epictetus (AD 55 – c.135)

Active listening is an art because it entails the use of all the senses. It seems like an easy concept to grasp, but it is a skill that takes time to master, as people are natural procrastinators. Thus, in a conversation, few people listen and stay in the moment. Instead, most people think of the future, i.e., what to respond, and how to respond to it.

Active listening involves having a bird's eye view on what is being said and reading all the undercurrents to the information being given. The communication process consists of a lot of nonverbal cues, and only a person adept in active listening can get all the information. Active listening also helps a person know when to respond, how to react, and what to reply. It is a skill that promotes cohesiveness and understanding, as very few arguments can arise from information that is adequately communicated and adequately received.

There is no formula for active listening, but there are steps that can be used to ensure that one becomes good at the art of active listening. Thus, one has to use methods that can help them be better listeners continually. Even if one thinks they are good listeners, it does not hurt to brush up their skills once in a while.

PAY ATTENTION

Active listening is not the same as hearing. Hearing is a purely physical process, where sound enters the ear, and nerves pass the information to the brain. Once there, the data can be processed or selectively passed to the subconscious. It all depends on what is paying attention to. Active listening involves actively choosing to understand the information being shared and have an attitude to interpret it. Thus, care has to be paid, so that active listening can take place.

To pay attention, one has to choose to listen. It means that a person has to focus on the speaker, do away with things that cause distractions. It can be achieved by making eye contact and giving complete attention to them. It also means that one has to move away from distractions such as noise, and anything that can take their mind off the speaker.

ASK FOR CLARIFICATION

Perception is different from communication. One can pass on a message, but what matters is how it is received. Therefore, clarification is essential, so that information can be received the way it is intended. One way to ask for clarification is to restate what has been said. In case the message was misperceived, the speaker will correct it. It also ensures that one pays attention and encourages the speaker to open up more.

Phrases like "what I understand from this is" should be used to make sure that the message is received well, and there is no mistake in the perception.

USE ALL SENSES

Look at body language, intonation, eye contact, and any behavior being projected, as they communicate a lot. Communication is not only verbal, and a lot can be understood from the way the message is passed. The tone of voice, choice of words, body language all communicate, and the listener will gain a lot from paying attention to this.

A change in tone can indicate that someone is lying or nervous. Crossed arms indicate defensiveness, avoiding eye contact can mean the speaker is shy or intimidated. Such information can help one know when to respond, how to react, and what to respond to.

MAINTAIN NEUTRALITY

Emotional intelligence is essential when communicating; one must be informed of their biases and opinions so that the art of active listening can be developed.

When communicating, it is essential to remain grounded. Getting defensive will impede the communication process. As much as people hate critics, one should be open to it, and understand that they are bound to be criticized from time to time.

Sensitive topics such as religion, politics should not be addressed first. They have the potential of bringing friction, which can derail a problem, due to their high level of sensitivity. Thus, one should not let such an instance derail a topic, as objectivity has to be maintained. In case it gives rise to tension, one should be able to change the subject to something less sensitive.

To avoid getting emotional, one should acknowledge that there are differing schools of opinions, and at times people have to agree to disagree. As adults, people do not have to agree on everything, but they can respect the fact that everyone has their own opinions. Thus, to avoid getting emotional, one has to agree to disagree and let some things go.

LISTEN

Let someone finish their train of thought before butting in and giving one's opinion. Moreover, one should listen entirely and take time to digest the information before evaluating the information provided. It is common for people to get distracted and start thinking of what to respond to before the speaker finishes what they are saying. It is paramount that one has to avoid this type of distraction because it prevents them from genuinely listening to the other person.

SILENCE

Bouts of silence when communicating allows time for one to digest the information given. It also provides room for evaluation of knowledge and time for a person to identify their biases, and how they might be affecting the listening process. Thus, silence should be used as a tool to sharpen the listening process and promote communication.

During a volatile interaction, silence can be an instrument that is used to bring tensions down. It can also be used to diffuse a conversation that is not productive. It enables parties involved to assess the chat and assess whether it is still within the objectives set.

Silence is usually seen as awkward during a conversation, but it can be essential to improve listening as a tool for communication.

USE ENCOURAGERS

Use prompts to encourage the other person to open up more. The prompts should be minimal so that the listening process is not impeded. Examples include; 'oh,' 'uh-uh' and 'then?'

Prompts indicate to the speaker that the listener is following what they are saying, and is genuinely interested in what they have to say. Thus, it encourages them to open up more. The listener also pays attention to what is being said because they take an active role in the conversation by encouraging the other person to open up more.

RESTATE

Every now and then, one is supposed to repeat what they have understood in their own words. This ensures that there is no mistake in what has been understood. It is essential to restate because at times, what is said, and what has been understood are different things.

For instance, one can say "what I understand is..." to indicate how they understood a concept. Parroting is not encouraged because it will not show how a person understood something.

REFLECT

Reflection enables the listener to take in the speaker's words. It also helps to connect the body language and other nonverbal cues to verbal communication. Thus, instead of just restating the information, one should take time to reflect the message, and take into account emotions, their background, and why they have the opinion that they have.

Reflection also enables one to make linkages with the information given. At times, one can make a comment, which can be connected to another piece of information. The information does not have to be from that conversation; it can be from a conversation previously had, or from another source.

Reflection is the right way for one to identify their bias, and how it affects the communication process, and decide how to do away with it.

USE 'I' MESSAGES

During active listening, putting feelings into words helps the speaker be objective. When communicating, one might not be aware of the body language they are projecting. This is especially true if they are talking about something sensitive to them. Thus, putting feelings brings objectivity to the conversation.

For instance, a person can say, "I can see that dancing makes you happy..." Such emotional labeling helps a person is more objective because the person can now describe how it makes them happy, and why it makes them happy.

VALIDATE

Be nonjudgmental to the way the speaker is feeling and validate their emotions. Listen with empathy, and understand why they think the way they think. At times, people get extreme emotions from trivial things, and it is okay, as people are entitled to feel, however, they think about issues that affect them.

Validation does not mean that one has to open up about their experiences. The goal is to listen and respond that their feelings are seen, and it is okay to have such feelings. In the communication process, this helps a person open up more.

REDIRECT

Sensitive topics can lead to aggression, raised voices, or anger. These are emotions like any other, and a person is entitled to them. Thus, instead of making someone feel bad for their feelings, it is better to redirect and talk about something that is not as sensitive.

It can be a brief discussion of a neutral topic, so that the tensions drop, then reverting to the question under discussion after that. If the speaker does not calm down, one can redirect and talk about something else entirely.

AVOID SUING COMMUNICATION BLOCKERS

Communication blockers make the speaker unable to pass on their points effectively. Thus, they should be avoided at all costs.

'Why' questions make people defensive because they feel like their validity is being questioned. Thus, they should be avoided.

Giving quick reassurances, before a person finishes expressing their point is not advised, because it they will not pass on the information effectively

Another communication blocker is advising the speaker. The goal is to listen and not advise someone unless the speaker asks for advice. Therefore, refrain from giving advice and actively listen.

Digging for information is another communication blocker. People are intelligent and can tell when a person is genuinely listing to them or is digging for information. Once they realize that the listener is doing for information, they clam up and stop communicating. Thus, for effective communication, avoid digging for information, in the pretense of active listening.

Patronization makes a person feel small and prevents them from communicating effectively. Thus, statements like "you poor thing" should be avoided so that the speaker feels equal to the listener.

One should not preach because it prevents proper communication. Thus, instances where the listener advices the speaker on what they should do it wrong unless they are asked to do it.

Interruptions should be intelligently made. Frequent breaks indicate that one is not interested in what is being communicated and impedes the whole communication process.

BE COURTEOUS

Have good manners when communicating. It indicates that the message is essential, and one is more likely to talk more to someone with polite behavior.

Statements like "excuse me', 'pardon me' should be used appropriately, and as stated before, they should be used sensibly to avoid frequent interruptions. They also indicate that someone is following the conversation actively.

QUESTIONING

Learn how to use questions to get the most out of conversations. For instance, leading questions can be used to make a person open up more. Open-ended questions are exploratory and delve deeper into an issue. Close-ended questions should be used when one wants to find out specific answers. Reflective questions help the speaker clarify information for the listener so that perception is not an issue.

Question is art during the listening process, and using the wrong type of question can lead to poor communication. The right kind of question indicates that one is a part of the conversion process.

It can be best described as a way to pass or receive information while considering one's actions. It includes taking into account

a person's steps, how they perform the steps, why they perform the activities, and the effect the steps have on other people. This type of self-awareness makes it easier for people to communicate and connect with other people. For any kind of relationship, emphatic communication is paramount, because it will enable the people in the partnership to identify with the feelings of the other person and communicate in a way that does not affect them negatively.

Emphatic communication makes it easier for one to express their feelings, ideas, and have a better chance of correctly responding to other people. It is an important skill to have, because it improves a person's ability to perform, at the same time enhancing other people's ability to function. Thus, it increases efficiency, friendliness, and effectiveness.

ENACTING EMPHATIC LISTENING IN A RELATIONSHIP

ASK QUESTIONS

To start a conversation, it is best to start by asking questions. The type of questions that are proposed as a conversation opener has to be neutral. This means that sensitive topics such as religion, politics, and gender have to be steered clear of. Asking questions ensures that a person considers the feelings of the other person first, and quickly learns their opinion on topics that are not as neutral.

AVOID JUDGMENTS

Every person on earth has a bias, and this is especially true when it comes to sensitive topics. Thus, to enact emphatic communication, one should avoid judging. One should listen keenly, and refrain from judging the other person at all cost. The other person in the relationship should feel like they are being listened to, and their point of view is being understood. Simply put, when communicating with someone, the listener should be able to walk a mile in the other person's shoes, and understand their point of view. In case there are arguments, they should be presented in a manner that is not judgmental.

PAY ATTENTION

There is nothing as unnerving as talking to someone who is not actively paying attention to the communication process. It makes a person lose interest and not open up as much as they want to. Thus, secure communication should be achieved by paying attention to the person speaking, be it in a group or a private setting. Distractions such as noise, phones, and other gadgets should be done away with, and the speaker is given undivided attention. It will enable the listener to identify the feelings of the speaker by reading the body language and respond accordingly.

REFRAIN FROM GIVING UNSOLICITED ADVICE

A popular pitfall to emphatic communication is giving advice or sharing one's point of view, even when the speaker has not sought it. At times, all a person wants is to be listened to. Giving advice that has not been asked for impedes this process, and the person will not be able to communicate their feelings effectively.

Thus, for empathic communication to occur, refrain from giving advice, unless the speaker directly asks for it. Additionally, sharing one's opinion on a subject is good. however, it communicates to the speaker is that the listener is self-centered, and does not consider the feelings of other people. At times, giving advice can generate resistance from the other party, and they stop communicating what they wanted to pass on. Thus, the objective of the conversation should be kept in mind at all times during the communication process.

USE THE LSF METHOD

The LSF method is a synonym for Listening-Summarizing-Follow up. It is a popular method used for achieving emphatic listening.

Listening involves actively paying attention to what someone is saying, and being in the moment. Active listening involves someone reading body language, the environment, and focusing on the matter in the message. It also means that the listener should be devoid of any distractions, and encourage the other person to open up more by using encouraging words, and asking questions when necessary. It is the first step of the technique because it is how the message is passed on.

Summarizing can either be done verbally or non-verbally. When done verbally, it can be a discussion with the speaker to clarify if what was understood, what was intended to be passed along. Summarization can also be done in one's mind, as the communication process ensues. It indicates that the listener has understood what has been said, the way it was intended. Keywords have to be used during the summarization process so that the listener can know that the main message was passed along. Depending on the situation, it is better to summarize verbally, so that any clarifications can be made.

Follow-up is whereby connections are made in the information given. For instance, a person can start a conversation by talking about one thing, and then link it up with something else. Follow up allows the listener to get clarification on how the linkages occur, and if what has been understood was what was meant to be communicated. It can also be to make connections with other things that are not part of the conversation. During follow up, it is essential to make sure that the goal of the communication process is kept in mind.

When using this method to enact emphatic communication, it is paramount that a person's emotions are considered, and acknowledged loudly. It makes the speaker see that the listener can relate or understands their point of view. Thus, a speaker can say, "I see this upsets you" to the listener when he says something that is upsetting to them.

SILENCE

Silence is powerful, especially in a conversation. It makes sure the listener can take in what has been said, and digest it, and give time for summarization. It helps the listener understand what the other person is trying to say and give room for the other person to organize their thoughts.

Short bouts of silence can be used to enact emphatic communication because they are a way for the listener to understand what the speaker is saying. It also gives room to a person to do away with their biases, and get the point from the other person's point of view, according to their background. Thus, silence during a conversation should not be seen as awkward, but a practical way to ensure empathic communication.

Managing short instances of silence is a skill that takes time to master. Thus, the listener should practice it so that they do not become awkward or indicate the end of the conversation.

RAISE ATTENTION LEVELS BY SELF-DETACHMENT AND DECREASING SELF-CENTRALIZATION

Seeing a point from someone else's point of view or experience is hard, and has to be learned. Thus, to increase attention, one has to detach themselves from their experiences and biases, and pay attention to the other person. It helps a person be in the moment, and solely understand what is being said at the moment.

Self-centeredness is an inherent human trait because it helps people survive. It helps people identify what is right for them and assist in the decision making process. However, it can impede empathic communication because one will be blind from the other person's reality. Therefore, self-decentralization should occur, and the existence of the other interculotor should be more critical. It is the only way that emphatic communication can occur.

Self-detachment and decentralization increase attention levels, when listening, one will not be making connections to the information given to their own lives. Instead, the listener will understand the information provided, free of bias or judgment.

READ THE SPEAKER

People might communicate one thing and mean the other. It happens to the nest of us, especially when we are nervous, or afraid of judgment. However, body language does not lie and will always betray what the speaker wants to say. This is why the listener should read the speaker.

A listener should be keen on the emotions that are behind what is being said. It will help in the emphatic communication process because the listener will be able to relate to the feelings that the speaker has. It will also help when giving responses, as the speaker will understand how to provide the answers.

Reading the body language also helps one understand the information that is being left out. Some information is tough to let out, but one might let out snippets of it. It is up to the listener to read between the lines and assure the speaker that he understands what is trying to be communicated.

This skill helps in the dynamic communication process because it puts one in the shoe of the speaker. It improves the effectiveness and connections made during the communication process. The speaker is more likely to open up when they are always reassured that their message is reaching home.

TAKE ACTION

Emphatic communication is meeting the needs of the other person. Thus, after being communicated to, one should take action and meet the other person at the point of their needs. It does not have to be the right action, but any activity that would help them overcome their situation.

A person might communicate that they do not seem to get a hold of their finances. An action that can be taken is teaching them simple methods of saving, referring them to someone who can help them. The most important part is their opinion has to be sort on which option is the best and let them make that decision for themselves.

In a relationship, empathy should not only be practiced when there is a crisis. It should be something that should be done at all times. Therefore, in every conversation held, one should be able to see the point from the other person's point of view, in any situation. Judgments should not be commonplace, and one should strive to widen their perspective on many issues.

Actions help build emphatic communication because they communicate that a person is reliable, and the listener is likely to communicate the next time they have an issue.

UNDERSTAND THAT PERCEPTION IS EVERYTHING

Psychology states that empathy involves communication and perception. Communication can occur at any time, but perception is very important, especially when one wants to build an emphatic connection.

People often understand what they want to, depending on their experiences and background. Thus, what is being communicated might not be what will be understood. Stephen Covey once said that "Many do not even listen with the intent to understand; they listen with the intent to reply." Ideally, many people are either speaking or are listening with the intent to reply. Therefore, conversations are like monologues because they are from one person's point of view.

Perception is everything because it develops emphatic communication. It enables a person to understand what is going on inside another human being, and this helps any action taken henceforth to be from another person's point of view. It also ensures productive conversations take place because it will be from the point of view of each person involved.

Perception also prevents conflict because of the understanding that needs to take place in the course of the conversation. Thus, to ensure empathic communication, one should make perception of their priority, and understand that there is always more to what is seen or being said.

CONNECT WITH THE ENVIRONMENT

Everyone needs to learn, and also has something to teach others. Thus, a person should make it their goal to connect with people in the background. It broadens a person's point of view and develops their ability to see life from different perspectives. Being closed in is a limitation, and dramatically impedes a person's communication skills.

Connection with other people develops empathic communication because it helps one to see that people have a lot in common, and everyone has a struggle. It reminds one that everyone needs to be cared for and be helped.

CHAPTER 4: HOW TO MAKE AN IMPACT THROUGH COMMUNICATION

Communication, in the business and social worlds, isn't just for conveying messages with clarity for the sake of it; it's a call to action. Brilliant ideas and thoughts cannot sell unless they are communicated in a persuasive manner that builds the consumers' need and confidence to venture into them. Impactful communication is about saying what is essential just when it matters most. It is the impression that your audience wants to get to rise to your call with urgency.

Better communication precedes better results. It facilitates change. It creates a compelling vision for the team and raises their level of collaboration. It stirs up the audience, makes them revaluate themselves and become self-aware for enhanced productivity. For the communication to be impactful, it must be intentional, have a central message, and be considerate of the receiver. It should engage the receiver, be clear and transformational.

At the most ordinary levels, communication blends visual, verbal, literal, and visceral content into a multi-sensory message. With some effort at enhancing impartation capability, the message can soon be transformed into actions that yield desired results. We suggest the following methodology for how you can influence your audience to get at work toward the endeavor that you will bring them through impactful communication.

UNDERSTAND YOUR AUDIENCE

Be aware of your audience. Know their characteristics. Know the type of event, their average age, some individual profiles, their needs and preferences, and their consideration of certain things or aspects of the arrangement. Gather, in prior, certain details like title of the event, choice of venue, topics of discussion, selected speakers, dress code, venue arrangement and time of the event, duration of your session, and the leading state of affairs or causative factors for the event.

These details describe the binding circumstances that bring you and your audience together. They, in a way, define both of you and your expectations of message content and how it should be packaged, presented, and delivered. It may not be possible to capture all of these details. However, the more of them you obtain in preparation and actual presentation, the closer you come to an understanding with the audience, aligning yourself and readily bonding with them.

You aspire to resonate with them, easily turn them up and retain their thoughts and feelings the whole While. This is without using a lot of energy on either side when you're live on stage. It is called customization—you capitalize on the customer resource and optimize on it and for their sake.

STICK TO THE NEED

This is important. Sometimes, the more and more you talk, the less and less you say. But what's required of you is to be relevant with your message start to the end. What's the theme of the conversation? What specific aspects are you addressing?

How far are you going in expounding on them? Are the facts binding to each other? How do they sum up to the focal message you are putting across? Do they answer the questions the audience is asking on their minds?

What story are you giving alongside the facts? Is it realistic? Does it highlight the issues of concern? And of the points of the solution, does it enhance their understandability? Are the solutions practicable? Does the story inspire hope at the very end? To stick to the need is to be relevant. You preempt the pertinent questions about the topic and answer them during the conversation. In doing that, be specific and detailed. Be time-conscious and create meaning for it in the value of the content you present.

ZOOM IN ON THE POINTS

Only enough detail is enough. All available time is enough for only that. Come out clearly on what your intention is and let the audience flow with you on that. Construct your sentences so as to expose their means as explicitly as possible. Not every point needs to be explained. Distinguish between the points. Add layers to your message. Adding layers means begin from a low level where everyone understands, and there, give the

foundational facts. Then go on to build on them toward the newer tougher ones, in a systematic way that is quick to understand.

Being focused doesn't mean you give little detail. Set a pace that is comfortable for both you and the audience. Be relaxed and considerate enough to know when the audience wants you to move on or explain further on the specific point being addressed at every moment. If you turn out to be over-exclusive, then you will end up not making sense throughout the session, and you don't want to get there. But it can be interesting how you get them to see your perception from their viewpoints. You zoom in on the points for their eyes to see from their positions what you see from your position.

MOVE YOURSELF TO MOVE THE AUDIENCE

What package of yourself and the surrounding, beyond the message in its essence and meaning, have you assembled to offer to your audience? Or are you a plain speaker? How are you amplifying your message? Are you affected by the calls and responses for the conversation? You need to realize that for the whole period of preparation for and execution of message presentation, you are exercising a form of leadership. Besides, if you do not give due consideration to your whole preparedness, the dynamics of the communication might work against you, such that the audience gives precedence to the implied messages than to the express one.

Make meaningful connections with your audience and transform them to your ideal audience. Be compelling. Make an intriguing entry point and invoke your conversation skills and bodily cues to raise and communicate your level of concern and involvement in the topic. Engage the audience for real-time interaction and feedback where necessary. Be present in the moment as you journey along from experience to experience, with an underlying sense of hopefulness and humor through it all.

You have the stage. You have the moment. And this is supposed to be one of the opportunities, not the last you have to voice your take on issues and take a stance in a way that is unique only to you. It takes courage. It takes skill. It takes commitment. This is not the last. There's more to come. And not just the message but you too need to be exceptionally memorable, especially for this event. Show your creativity in how you analyze the depths and widths of the problem, organize the message, and prepare and present yourself for conversation. How smartly can you respond to sudden unexpected mishaps?

Stand out from the rest and be distinctive. It feels great. Present the better version of yourself looking different sounding different and feeling different from everyone. Think of yourself as an ambassador for what you speak, and push your expectations and effort for that job to the next level. It is a competitive world in every aspect of life, and you have this chance to show yourself the better preferable option in this issue as well.

BE REAL AND TRUE

Be yourself. What strange extremes do you want to go to pass your message across effectively? Are you expending undue excess energy to perform this task? Are you dramatic? Putting on performance is being dishonest with yourself and others. It does not take long before the audience realizes that you are exaggerating your personality, and when they do, they soon withdraw their trust from you and refuse to accept your message as well.

Honesty is the best policy and key to positive and profitable relationships. Mind what you say and how you say it. Inject your personality and opinions in a natural, effortless manner in order to resonate and be relatable. Avoid pretense. Be authentic to the extent of your considerations and capabilities. Know your esteem and present and speak of yourself as such. Do not compromise your stakes in matters. Acknowledge your worth and show that respect two-way.

MANIFEST YOUR VALUES

Do you believe in hard work, honesty, trustworthiness, teamwork, transparency, accountability...? Inculcate them in your presentation. While you may not mention and justify yourself against each, but their influence on the final presentation that you make must be factored. What are your values as enablement for doing what you do? How much of that is manifest in this specific assignment? What kind of person will the audience describe you to be after the presentation?

Your values are silent, yet the audible soul of the message. You need to prove your value by being true to these values. When your cues and message supplement each other, the audience naturally trusts you and thinks of you as reliable. Congruence on your side as the speaker translates into eloquence to the listeners. And a blend of this gift with your core values is what makes people find you to be consistent – outside as on the inside, over and over. There's no better way to prove yourself in life than stay true to your values in whatever you engage in word or deed.

ADD COLOR

Whatever ideas you say to the human mind verbally or non-verbally all crystallize on the brain as steel pictures. The details of shape and speed add dimension, arrangement, and motion which the brain understands as a series of images played in a certain order within a certain time period. Color adds emotion and feeling, and that's what excites the mind. When you tell the audience to imagine, they see colored images and react to the intensity of color and associated activity.

You need to be thoughtful with the images, colors, fonts, wardrobe etcetera so that the kind of imagery you create is quickly comprehensible to the audience and relatable to the focal message you're putting across. You want to use the two to tell one story in a more powerful way. Mind your choice of words. How would you present a negative fact in a rather positive way? Where's your sense of humor? Do not entirely depend on verbal content nor be jumbled with your presentation. Try and progress in an orderly way for things to flow smoothly. Be visual.

TOUCH IT AND FEEL IT

How do you touch up the ideas and their meanings and implications? Combine facts and figures with personal stories and conceptual metaphors. What do the numbers mean theoretically, and how does that feel in real life? If you have your experience of it, then describe how it felt like working for and achieving the final result, and what that meant for you. How would you wish for people to go about it more conveniently subsequently?

Share knowledge with emotional resonance. Be careful, however, not to turn the discussion into self-glorification as it may not be received well and that may distort the importance of your message. Dry statistics and shiny objects alone throughout a whole communication period are meaningless, not for lack of fact but lack of interfacing with humans. What we don't relate with, we don't make meaning of, however big or small.

GATHER VIEWS

Reach out to others for their opinions about the topic you are about to address. Weigh their views against your own and find the best way to organize your content. Your inquiries should not only concern with content but also with the methods of delivery. A right message needs to be translated and transferred equally well, for it to be effectively good. Share your execution plan with a few others again and note their observations.

Ask for honest feedback and consider each of them before you prepare your final presentation. Part of feedback consideration is to ensure that what is said is what is heard, and what's said is what's purposed. Open up to your friends' influences, and borrow some of their experiences, for example, in your text. Mind all your preparations and get clear guidance where it is needed. You can perform demo presentations to psyche yourself up for the event.

Many people fear attending interviews. They do not know how to prepare themselves for the interviews adequately. They then end up presenting themselves as not being the ideal candidates for the job when, in fact, they could be best suited for the opportunity. And sometimes they know it at heart. But there is no second chance to create a great first impression. So, what should one do to convince the panel that s/he is best suited for the job?

RESEARCH ON INSTITUTIONAL BACKGROUND INFORMATION

This may not be easily perceived to be a part of the interview preparation. But it definitely rewards one who works at it by giving them an edge above the others who ignore it. Review the job and interview invitation posts and see how much you can gather beforehand about the company. Visit their website as well and read the history of the institution and how it has grown to the current status.

Review the mission statements, vision statements, motto, values, guiding principles, the organizational structure, and how the position you are applying for fits in. This information will make you more confident as you go for the interview.

PREPARE FOR STANDARD QUESTIONS

Certain standard questions are usually asked in most interviews. Prepare for such ones in advance. For instance, questions about your leadership skills will normally start like 'WHAT WOULD YOU DO IN THE EVENT THAT...?' or 'CONSIDER A SITUATION WHERE... WHAT WOULD YOU PROPOSE?' or 'HOW HAVE YOU DEALT WITH... IN YOUR CAREER LIFE BEFORE?' or 'DESCRIBE OR PAINT TO US A PICTURE OF WHEN...'

Such questions, however dynamic they may be, mainly draw answers from instances you had interacted with before in your career or private life and how you handled them. Do not stop at just that, but mention how the experiences enhanced your growth in your private and career life. What consequence did the outcome have on the institution where you were then?

PREPARE YOUR QUESTIONS

Having the background information about the institution and having prepared for the standard questions, use them to prepare a few questions. Your questions should focus on filling in the gaps in the information gathered. Try finding out how they have been able to post their trending results. Think of questions that, when answered, will help you to tap into the company's prevailing resources to achieve more of its objectives.

Your questions should require short answers or tips. It is a counter-interaction you purpose to create, not counter-interview. But you want to do it in a way that sets you apart from the rest. Also, mind any goals for your specific job and how they are perceived going into the future.

PRACTICE GOOD NON-VERBAL COMMUNICATION

Perhaps this is not just done in preparation for interviews alone, but for your effective general communications. Invest your time in training yourself on how to be congruent during your communications. Learn and practice positive body language. Also, learn about and avoid negative body language. Train yourself to purposefully assume postures to communicate good feelings and messages about you.

Symmetrical facial expressions, the movement of your head, the gesturing by your hands, the leaning forward, eye contact, the tonal variations, the short laughter, the short silences, and those thoughtful moments. Whatever you say verbally, with good practice, must be supplemented with your bodily language. This will portray your consistence and prove your trustworthiness, giving you an edge above the rest.

DRESS FOR THE JOB

How does the corporate world perceive professionals in this kind of job? How does this company want it? Most interview invitations do not require you to dress in a particular way. This is because they expect you to have some level of self and professional awareness. Are there any activities that you might participate in during the interview? Find that out from the invitation or draw from your previous interview experiences.

If you can, call and inquire how the company expects you to dress. If they are not keen on it, ask about the company culture. The point is the more you present yourself as identifying with the company culture and aware of your office literally, the more convincing you are. It demonstrates your willingness to enhance the image of the office and the company at large. It exudes your confidence already with the company and makes it look like there is more you would prove in performance if given the job.

ARRIVE IN TIME

Mark your check-in time or when the interview commences and arrive 15 to 30 minutes prior. This will allow you time to familiarize yourself with the venue, observe a few things that might be helpful for the interview, and relax as you focus your mind on it. Getting there on time is not advised because you might not be allowed time to tune in into the interview mood. You are also advised not to arrive more than 30 minutes earlier.

The aspect of time is perceived first in its property of scarcity. You are not sure there's a holding room while you wait for your turn, or even if so, maybe it was not desired for candidates to queue at the venue. It could be a strategy to ensure your time is not wasted at the venue. And you do not want to cause concerns at the reception in any of these ways. You may also be thought of as not being economical with your time spending a whole hour in the waiting room. If you are not sure what time to arrive and are concerned with the interview procedures, make a call and inquire for any elaborations before the due date.

REVIEW YOUR RESUME

This is a step that many want to take for granted or forget. They think it is self-authored about self and expect that they have grasped everything in their minds. But there is more to what is written in your resume than what is read by eye. The purpose of the review is to ensure you have internalized it adequately, and you can say anything about yourself in the light of it.

You do not want to appear strange to yourself when a panelist draws a query from your resume, and you do not understand or respond to it adequately. This point cannot be overemphasized.

LISTEN

From the onset, the job posting and interview invitation are saying something that might be crucial during the interview. The interviewer as well is, directly and indirectly, giving you some information which if you do not get, you might miss the opportunity. Where you need to acknowledge hearing, do so. It is equally important to observe the style and pace that the panel is creating for the interview, and match to them.

Lean in or sit upright to show interest in what is being said to or asked of you. Maintain adequate friendly eye contact to show your focus on what is being said. While it is necessary to nod, but do not overdo. Try as much as possible to hear every speaker right away so that you do not keep asking them to repeat themselves. However, seek clarity where you do not get it right away.

TALK ONLY ENOUGH

Do not talk too much. When responding to a question stick only to the relevant points. Make them brief and precise. The risk of trying to explain more about every point is that you end up digressing. And that can be disapproving. Remember, interview questions are more practical than academic. And you are not trying to prove your mastery of knowledge, but applied the skill. Precision and timekeeping need to be demonstrated to be a part of your skillset.

When narrating a certain situation and its effects, do not story-tell. Choose the specific moments where an effect is attached, or a lesson is drawn. Do not assume and skip relevant details, but understand that the panel is comprised of intelligent people who know what they want to hear from your statements. It may not be primarily what you say. Use technical terms. They are magic words that do the explanations on your behalf.

DO NOT BE TOO FAMILIAR

Recognize that you are in for an interview and not any other business or regular meeting. Most interview sessions discourage personal and social identity between the panelists and the interviewee. The interfacing between the two is the company business, and that is where communications and interactions must originate and terminate. However, you want to express yourself and your feeling during the interview, be mindful of the interviewers' demeanor, and, if to the most extreme, mimic just that.

MIND YOUR LANGUAGE

Use the official, and more precisely functional, professional language. You chose to attend the interview because you knew you could express yourself verbally in the required language. You have no other option but respect that. Depending on your training and job requirements, use relevant terminologies to show your communication capability in and deeper understanding of your discipline.

Avoid slang and racist, sexist, and politically and religiously intolerant words. Show respect to the subjects and objects of reference when you mention them in your communications. Feel free to infer from your social, economic, and religious experiences where necessary, but make sure that they are relevant and serve the right purpose for the interview.

HAVE MODERATION

Show a positive attitude toward the panel, for the interview exercise, toward the institution and its objectives, and toward the prospective job that you are in for. Strike a balance between confidence, professionalism, and modesty. Do not be overconfident. Equally, have a tolerance to retain your rational mind throughout the interview without coming under undue pressure.

Control your emotions. Consider carefully whether it is necessary to put on a performance and do it only when it serves to prove your capability without going overboard.

WORK ON YOUR ANSWERS

You know you can do the job. Whatever you present for and in your answers, and however you do it, you need to demonstrate this fact. Let the panel know, by seeing and listening to you, how well you articulate not just the queries raised but the forthcoming roles in your job. Make them believe that. Do not just narrate your understanding and knowledge in the profession. Blend them into the culture of the company and demonstrate how they will help advance the company targets.

ANSWER THE QUESTIONS

Ensure you understand what each question wants from you and focus your answers to adequately and precisely hit there. For instance, if asked to give a description of yourself, focus more on your values and how they will help you work for a difference in the company. Avoid being academic and historical. Say what you have in the present as a person and leader that can help you run the organization into a fruitful future. Avoid unnecessary details, and don't stick there for too long. Be careful though; answers too brief might imply that you are not interested in the interview and the opportunity consequently.

ASK QUESTIONS

What most candidates never imagine is the fact that not having questions for the panel might be a sign of disinterest in the company after all. Ask questions that show your interest in the company's business. Ask also so you may know whether it's the right place for you. Any informational gaps you need to be covered can be raised here. Ask about any challenges that face the position you are applying for.

DON'T APPEAR DESPERATE

Put on a confident face. Do not beg for employment. Everyone, including the interviewer, knows that you need the job. That's why you turned up for the interview. And what they demand of you are your values and attributes of strength and determination.

Appearing to be needy is appearing to be less and less confident, and that is disqualifying. Contain yourself. Keep your cool, and remain calm and confident.

DON'T SPEAK ILL OF YOUR FORMER EMPLOYER

Speak ill of you the previous company and panel knows it won't take long before you quit to go spoiling their name also elsewhere. Saying that the previous employer was great but you come here to add a certain dimension to your professional experience is more welcome.

Generally, negative statements elicit negative feelings, and positive statements elicit positive feelings towards you, not towards the subjects in your statements.

THANK YOU NOTE

After the interview, appreciate the panel for having had you. Further, reply to the email invitation for the interview in a formal way with a thank you statement. What goes around comes around.

CHAPTER 6: THE ART OF QUESTIONING

WHY QUESTIONING

We ask questions to:

- Gather information. The information helps us to learn more and add to our knowledge of something, solve problems, make informed and balanced decisions and understand each other clearly and at a deeper level
- Maintain control of a conversation. When you want specific information from a conversation, you become more assertive and ask questions leading the conversation in that direction
- Express our interest in the respondent. We want to find out more about them, and build a rapport with them, or show empathy to them, or just get to know them better

- Seek clarity on points. We want someone to come out clearly on what they are saying so that they are distinctly understood. This helps to reduce misunderstandings and make communication more effective
- Explore the personality of the respondent and what they are experiencing in life. We want to know their beliefs, their ideas and their attitudes, and any circumstances of difficulty that they may be enduring
- Test knowledge. You want to know whether you or the other person is adequately informed about something. Examinations do exactly this
- Spur further thoughts. You want someone to think deeper or differently about something. For instance, 'WHY DO YOU THINK NAIROBI IS THE CAPITAL CITY OF KENYA?'
- Include all members, encourage discussion on a particular point, and keep everyone's attention in a group discussion. For instance, asking participants to give more contributions, or even asking a specific one to speak on the point of discussion, etc.

HOW QUESTIONS ARE ASKED

In order for one to ask a question, you perform the following simple steps:

Establish the Purpose of the Question

First, know why you need to ask the question. Evaluate the kind of response you expect. The meaning you want to draw from the response. And what you want to do with what you make of it.

Select the Type of Question

Ask yourself whether the question is relevant to the person or group. Consider if it is the right time and how you want or expect them to respond.

Consider These Factors

Structure

Consider the circumstances under which you are asking the question and structure the question appropriately. For instance, you may need to introduce yourself. Or you may need the background to it. Or you may need to state the reason for the question. Or you may need to ask a few other questions ahead of or afterward.

Establishing the structure helps to run the conversation between the questioner and respondent smoothly.

Silence

The silence between 3 and 5 seconds is a powerful tool too by which a question can be delivered. Silence before a question emphasizes the message just delivered. Silence after a question prevents you from asking the next question as well as tells the respondent that a reply is required. A further silence after the reply has been given tells the respondent that more detail is required.

Participation

In a group scenario, you may want to involve as many participants as possible in the debate. For instance, a question may be redirected from an active participant to a quieter member. Though this doesn't mean the quiet member is forced to speak when they do not want to.

QUESTIONING METHODS

OPEN AND CLOSED QUESTIONS

Closed questions are questions that require a single word, very short or factual answers. The respondent is supposed to respond with definite stances and is not required to give details. If options are provided, then they are only a few or even if they are more, the respondent can only pick a few among them. Closed questions are best suited for testing one's understanding, concluding a discussion, making a decision or for frame-setting.

Frame setting is asking a question in such a manner that the respondents are forced to see the issue with a certain frame of mind. For instance, 'PLEASED TO MEET WITH THE VICE-CHANCELLOR OF THE INSTITUTIONS?' Closed questions must be avoided when the discussion is in full flow because if it can suddenly terminate the conversation. The respondent, feeling uncomfortable to respond to the question in the way you do not expect, might go quiet and result in awkward silence. Most closed questions begin with 'WHO...' or 'WHICH...' or 'WHERE...' or 'CHOOSE...' etc.

Open questions require long answers. The respondent tells their story in narrating an event, or how it occurred, or why it occurred. They are free to speak out their knowledge, opinion, and feeling about something without being restrained or confined. Open questions are used to develop an open conversation, for establishing more details as well as for finding opinions on issues. Most open questions begin with 'WHAT...' or 'WHY...' or 'HOW...' or 'DESCRIBE...' or 'IN YOUR...' etc.

FUNNEL QUESTIONS

Funnel questioning is a method that begins with general questions then drills down to more specific points in each. At each level, more and more details are inquired. This method helps the respondent to bring to mind more details about something or an event, and zoom in on the important details. Begin by asking closed questions then move on to more open ones as the conversation progresses.

Use this approach when you want to find out more details about a specific point. Also, when you are gaining more interest in someone or are trying to increase their confidence, then this is the method to use. See the following:

> YOU: YOU ATTENDED HIGH SCHOOL?
>
> RESPONDENT: YES.
>
> YOU: IN WHICH SCHOOL?
>
> RESPONDENT: HIMALAYAS.
>
> YOU: HIMALAYAS BOYS'.
>
> RESPONDENT: NO. ACTUALLY, HIMALAYAS MIXED.

YOU: OH, I SEE. SO, YOU TOOK COMPUTER STUDIES, IT WAS OFFERED IN THE SCHOOL EVEN THEN…, AS A SUBJECT AND THAT'S WHERE YOU REALIZED YOU HAD THIS PASSION FOR COMPUTERS.

RESPONDENT: YES.

YOU: AND YOU SCORED A GOOD GRADE IN THE SUBJECT, CREATING A WAY FOR YOU TO JOIN MACADAMIA SCHOOL OF COMPUTING AND ROBOTICS. TELL US MORE ABOUT THAT.

RESPONDENT: BLAH BLAH BLAH…

YOU: LET'S NARROW INTO THIS ROBOTICS SUBJECT. WHAT ESPECIALLY DID YOU DO WITH IT TO BECOME WHAT YOU ARE TODAY?

RESPONDENT: BLAH BLAH BLAH...

PROBING QUESTIONS

Probing questions are used to find out more details. You can do this by asking for an example that will help you understand the statement just made. You can also ask for additional information for clarification purposes. You can go further and inquire whether there's proof of what is said, and what the proof is. The word 'exactly' is used to make the respondent give as precise detail as possible.

Use this method to gain clarification and to ensure you have the whole story and that you understand it wholly. If you are interviewing a person who you think is trying to withhold or alter some details, then this is the method you use to extract information out of them.

WHAT EXACTLY WAS SAID IN THE LAST PARAGRAPH?

LEADING QUESTIONS

You use leading questions when you want to lead the responded in your direction of thinking without forcing them, nor them realizing or trying to resist. You may do that by beginning the question with an assumption, e.g., 'HOW EARLY DO YOU THINK HE WILL MAKE THERE?' This question supposes that he will make it there early. You can also lead by adding a personal appeal to agree at the end, often using a tag question, e.g. 'HE WILL GET THERE EARLY; DON'T YOU THINK SO?' The tag question suggests that the respondent agrees with the fact that he (subject in the sentence example) will get there early.

You can also phrase it such that the responded finds it easier to say yes, e.g. 'YOU WOULD LIKE ME TO SERVE YOU TEA INSTEAD. YES?' The respondent is forced to say yes, or otherwise explain himself out, which is more work which they, largely, will avoid. You can also choose to give two options, both of which make you happy. This method makes you get what you want, but the respondent is left to feel they had no choice to use to stop you. It can also be used to close a deal, e.g. 'NOW THAT ALL CONDITIONS ARE MET SHALL WE APPEND OUR SIGNATURES?'

This method should, however, not be overused or misused because it can be seen to be self-serving for you and harming the interests of others telling of you to be manipulative and dishonest.

RHETORICAL QUESTIONS

These are questions that do not require to be answered because they are basically statements phrased as questions. This method is quite pleasantly engaging for the audience. The audience is drawn to think by themselves and agrees with you rather than to be told. It is a good way of getting people to agree with your point of view. Rhetorical questions can be more powerful when used in a string.

WHO DOESN'T WANT TO TAKE THEIR KIDS TO SCHOOL? AND WHO DOESN'T LIKE IT WHEN THEIR CHILDREN EVENTUALLY FINISH SCHOOL AND GRADUATE WITH GOOD GRADES? AND WHEN THEY GET EMPLOYMENT AND COME HOME WITH THAT SHOPPING EVERY NEXT MONTH OF EVERY YEAR, WHAT BETTER FEELING CAN ONE GET THAN JOY AND CONTENTMENT?

USING QUESTIONING TECHNIQUES

The different questioning methods can be used independently or in combination, depending on how you want to lead the conversation. Below, we suggest the situations in which certain questioning methods would apply best.

LEARNING

Open questions help you to expand your coverage of topics while the closed questions will help you ascertain the validity of your understanding of the various facts about the topics. Where your understanding is shallow probe further to deepen it appropriately.

RELATIONSHIP BUILDING

Your counterpart is more likely to respond positively when you ask them about what they do or for their opinions. Do so in an affirmative way, and they will open up with more ease. For instance, 'SO TELL ME, WHAT HAVE YOU COME TO LIKE BEST ABOUT OUR OFFERS? 'Ask open questions and maintain an open dialog.

MANAGING AND COACHING

Rhetorical and leading questions are best suited in this situation. You make your suggestion using a leading question and ask them to agree with you in rhetorical questions. This combination helps the respondents to reflect and commit to your suggested courses of action.

AVOIDING MISUNDERSTANDING

When trying to avoid a looming misunderstanding whose consequences can be dire, use the probing technique to establish details of the causes. This method requires you to probe deeper and deeper into why every answer is being given. When the answers begin to make little sense or usefulness of the answers diminishes, then the likely corrective measure becomes quite obvious. The one advantage of this method is that it prevents hurried jump to conclusions.

DEFUSING A HEATED SITUATION

Use framed questions to make an angry person see more details about their grievance. This invokes their minds into action and distracts them from their feeling of sadness. It will also provide a window for you to see a practical way of intervening to make them feel better.

PERSUADING PEOPLE

Keep asking open questions that will help them see and embrace the reasons behind your point of view. Agreeing along with you, they feel positive to engage in what you ask of them willingly.

So, the art of questioning can be developed. By testing yourself in various situations, you will master the skill and nurture it to full development. In the closing remarks, it is important to allow your correspondents enough time to think and respond to your questions. Create a rapport and maintain that relationship throughout the discussion. Secondly, be a skillful thinker and a careful listener so that you understand what the answers really mean as intended by the corresponded. Finally, your body language and tonal voice will play a significant role in determining what kind of answers you get for the questions asked. Ask right and in the right manner, and you will get the right answers.

CHAPTER 7: PHONE CONVERSATION

One of the essential characteristics of achievement in business is the ability to converse by phone. Answering the handset is not a complex duty; however, using it in a business and in a specialized way is not easy.

Conversing with a client on the phone might often be a tricky mission. Without seeing a person's face, the messages might become mixed-up and meanings misread.

DISCLOSE YOUR IDENTITY

When people make calls, they should first introduce

themselves. Start by revealing your name and talking with a fine tone. However, make sure to uphold your pitch level. People might not see the person with whom they are conversing. The caller should not use many passionate words at the beginning.

So, it will facilitate to boost impressions regarding the caller and bring satisfaction for both parties.

CLARITY

The caller must avoid speaking too quick and mumbling. The receiver might not be conversant with the language used by the caller. As a consequence, it will assist the caller in putting across the message to the receiver correctly. Additionally, it will assist in reassuring the receiver.

CHOOSING WORDS

It is not correct to use teenager language with the boss or grandfather. The caller should know the individual who they are speaking with. At times the caller might not know the person who they are talking with. However, in the first phase of the call, the caller introduces themselves by revealing their names and title. Consequently, the caller should use their universal knowledge and apply appropriate language practices when they are conversing with other people over the telephone.

LISTEN KEENLY

The receiver should listen appropriately and enthusiastically before answering the caller. Or else they might not answer correctly and get their message accurately. Additionally, when the receiver is listening to the caller over the telephone, they should not disrupt them. Generally, interrupting while somebody is speaking is considered an offensive practice.

EXCELLENT AND EXPRESSIVE LANGUAGE

People make calls to somebody to express their messages and get a response. As a result, individuals have to apply fine and explanatory language to make suitable discussion. In addition, the language must be evocative and correctly flowing. Since language and tone is the only medium that people may utilize over the phone, it is appropriate to use excellent and descriptive language with meaningful information through the conversation.

CARRY A PEN AND A PAPER

It is constantly best to utilize a pen and paper before and during a call. While making a call, both the caller and the receiver may have to note down something. It might be a phone contact or home address. Or else the person making the call might have to waste their time and funds to buy a paper and a pen whilst calling, and it is not an excellent practice too.

UTILIZE SPEAKERPHONE WHEN NEEDED

It is easier for the caller because they might use their hands to multitask. On the other hand, for the receiver, it is like trying to listen to one voice through a hooted crowd of taxis.

USE OF TEXT MESSAGE TO COMMUNICATE

Using phone messages to organize where an individual is meeting somebody is a common use of text messaging by many people. However, organizing a physical meeting with somebody is not carried out as regularly as calling. On the contrary, only a few people who send text organize a meeting at least once a day.

Receiving and sending messages has one specific advantage as compared to voice calls. With the appropriate handset settings put in place, text messages may convey information silently between the sender and the receiver. The majority of people say they take advantage of the ability to noiselessly generate and send messages to the desired people. On the other hand, very few people who send text say they do this daily.

As compared to voice calls, a moderately smaller number of people receive and send text messages for job purposes on their telephone. On the contrary, the majority of people rarely sent a work-related message. It implies that many work-related communications are channeled through voice calls.

Texting is less likely to be embraced for long conversations regarding individual matters than voice calls. On the other hand, text message users make distance calls to talk about a specific essential issue. On the contrary, a few people use messages for distance communication.

Not astonishingly, people who send and receive huge numbers of messages daily are likely to text regularly for all-purpose. This is as compared to the person who sends and receives fewer texts. In a comparable vein, people who make and receive high numbers of calls on their phones daily are expected to send and receive messages for several purposes.

For most categories of businesses, the phone plays a key part in daily operations. It is as a result of business persons needing them to contact dealers, business acquaintances, and clients. Phones are helpful because they enable communication with clients by permitting them to transact business related activities at any time of the day. As vital as the telephone is, it is essential that businesses distinguish the difference between what is considered excellent and terrible phone etiquette. They must understand that how they call customers and business friends on the phone shall either depict them positively or negatively. In the hands of a badly trained worker, administrator, or company owner, phone communication might have a tremendously negative consequence on the business.

Receiving business calls at work comprises a different approach to a usual, non-business call. When clients call the company, they expect complete concentration. As a result, they do not desire to be kept waiting and need timely answers.

When a call is picked well and clients are happy with the service; they will do business again with the company. For a company, the phone is frequently the initial and only point of getting in touch with some clients. It might primarily make or break a company affiliation. That is why a lot of organizations employ specialized answering services nowadays.

Because opening impressions are permanent, and frequently such impressions are contacted on the phone, the client will make a judgment of the business by how the discussion went with the spokesperson. If the receiver is able to impress callers, then the company will have permitted clients to shop around. This implies that the company has given new customers a basis and an assurance to do business.

When a company spokesperson is prepared before taking a client's calls, it indicates the willingness of a company to do business with the caller. On the other hand, keeping the clients waiting and speaking offensively might critically damage the status of the company.

Phone etiquette is important in competitive business because if the company does not do it right, the client might choose from another alternative. Phone etiquette is an essential part of client service. Frequently, customers call for return business since they are familiar with the manner in which the company functions. If the receiver is not polite, timely, and well-informed, the company is not giving the customer any reason to come back.

Many people around the world appreciate that their phones make them feel satisfied and help them get in touch with friends and relatives. On the contrary, a number of phone users express annoyance with their handset for the disturbance it generates.

DISADVANTAGES OF USING PHONES AT WORK

A number of upcoming companies have a vested curiosity in watching calls made during job hours. It might help decrease personal calls and offer information they might use to coach workers on communicating with customers and business associates more efficiently. Creating a call-monitoring structure on a conventional land-line system is relatively easy. However, it is not characteristically possible for small businesses to install such expensive equipment. The major shortcoming of phone communication is that it disrupts the work flow both in the shape of individual calls and job-related calls. It increases the view that the employees are constantly prone to accept calls at the expense of committing to work.

As every employee may agree, one of the difficulties of telephone calls of any sort is that they disturb whatever an individual is doing. Adding up cell phones to work adds one more disturbance. A worker who has to stop job tasks during the day to respond to phones might suffer from reduced productivity. It might cause the worker to ignore deadlines or put in additional hours to finish projects on time.

Employees, who take job-related calls outside regular job hours, whether on a company-provided handset or an individual cell phone, might feel a disparity between their work and individual lives. That is one of the disadvantages of cell phone communication. It might be tricky for a worker to enjoy time away from work when their duties fall over into family, communal, and break time. It might increase worker stress, reducing the capability of workers to manage job tasks successfully.

CHAPTER 8: COMMUNICATION AND SOCIALIZATION

Communication and socialization is an individual's awareness and capability to comprehend the intentions of other people. People articulate their personal intentions significantly and correctly by interacting with other people in their surroundings.

Communication ability is the key to increasing friendships and constructing a sturdy social support set-up. They as well help an individual to take care of their personal needs while being considerate of the needs of other people. Additionally, People are not born with excellent communication skills. Like any other ability, communication skills are cultured through trial and error and constant practice.

WHAT TO SAY WHEN YOU MEET SOMEONE FOR THE FIRST TIME

It might be fairly an anxious time when a person is meeting somebody new. Often people might doubt what they ought to speak. It does not matter if it is an appointment, a new job associate, a company meeting, or somebody people meet in social circumstances. People might be stuck for what to speak when meeting somebody for the first time. But, all of these circumstances present an individual a chance to strike up a discussion and begin a rapport on superior terms.

THE GREETING

The primary step to take when meeting somebody is to smile and salute them. It should be followed by an introductory part. A smile will calm down the new person and make them appear welcome. In addition, the other individual also relaxes and feels warmly connected to the new person.

USE THE SITUATION

People meet for a reason, whether that is a gathering or a celebration. People may discover some links between them to converse about during such an occasion. For instance, if individuals are at a business meeting, they could inquire how long the other individual has worked for the business. Or at a social gathering, an individual may inquire how they know the crowd.

Beyond that, a person could employ their physical setting to discover something to speak about. So, a person might ask something concerning the other person's trip or comment upon the interior decoration. Ask their judgment regarding something and prove that you are concerned about what they suppose.

KEEP IT LIGHT

When meeting someone, people should keep their remarks light and encouraging. Consequently, they will get a reaction that is identical to the impression they elicit. People should not voice any strong judgments until they know the other individual well. People could likely upset the ones they are meeting for the first time with such comments. Keep divisive subjects for a later planned meeting.

RELAX

People have a basis to be insecure when meeting somebody for the first time since in these circumstances they have by no means met them either. They are equal as they both come in the situation fresh and new.

Even though people have to be cautious not to upset new persons, they should not feel the need to pretend.

MANNERS

Even if the person has insulted somebody at the first meeting, they may save the reputation. Apologize and let it be recognized that it was not intentional to cause the offense. If new people might see that the confession is genuine and that the person meant no offense, they will be okay with the explanation and not hold a resent.

NEVER OVERSTAY THE WELCOME

If an individual is meeting somebody for the first time, they might desire to keep the meeting fairly short. Or at least plan some type of exit tactic if the deal is not going as planned. Be certain to be grateful to them for their time in talking to you and depart on excellent terms. As a result, they are left with a fine perception of the person. This might leave the door open to speak with them once more. Consequently, what to speak when meeting somebody for the first time must be light, open, and welcoming. It must not explore too extremely into private issues nor reveal too much. It is sufficient to smile and be open and concerned with the other individual and make light discussions regarding the agenda of the meeting.

AVOID UNHELPFUL REMARKS

If an individual is going to meet somebody who complains, the person shall kill the relationship even before initiating it. Though the above account could be right, they are better left unspoken in a common or business situation.

AVOID MONEY ASSOCIATED ISSUES

The sum of money an individual makes is a private subject. It is offensive to ask somebody a query regarding their income. If the person is curious or it is significant that they know much he or she makes they might research information regarding wages on the internet.

AVOID RELIGIOUS OPINIONS

In spite of how spiritual or non-religious an individual is. People must shun asking queries regarding religion when meeting somebody on the first day. Except if the person is at a religious gathering or a member of the church.

AVOID QUERIES REGARDING SEXUAL ORIENTATION

This actually is a private question; it might make somebody scratchy and might trigger sexual annoyance.

AVOID SUBJECTS CONCERNING PHYSICAL APPEARANCE

Keep away from commenting on private appearances or possessions, even if it is constructive. Even after people get to know each other, they should be cautious about what they speak. Physical remarks are best shunned. An individual could offer genuine work-related admire instead.

AVOID INFORMATION REGARDING HEALTH AND POVERTY

If an individual is experiencing something complex, it might be persuasive to share it with the new partner, but it is completely unsuitable. If a person is facing severe health matters that must be discussed with the employer it should be well-thought through. Precise details regarding physical condition and hardship must be avoided during the first meeting.

AVOID EGOTISTICAL CONVERSATIONS

"I" is the negligible note in the alphabet, so do not make it the biggest word in the expressions. The most excellent technique to shun "I centric" discussion is to demonstrate a genuine interest in other people by and listening keenly and asking the right questions.

THINGS TO DO TO BE REMEMBERED

AMUSE YOURSELF

The tip is, as an individual always feel entertained. You are the key because you do not do it for other people. Consequently, everybody is welcome to link with you and perceive what is comical. However, do not try to make other people express amusement. If the audience gets entertained it is okay, if not, then the speaker has fun on their own.

By doing that the listener gets attracted to the speaker. As a result, the listener becomes interested in why the speaker has so much fun. Everybody desires to be in an entertaining community. The act of amusement adds value to people's lives. On the contrary, no individual fails to recall the person who made them smile. However, everybody forgets the joker who tried to be humorous for several hours.

BE FRANK, CONTROVERSIAL AND GENUINE

People cannot be recalled by constantly playing it safe. Everybody desires to be remembered, and most individuals avoid disagreement. However, by avoiding disagreement, people position themselves in the center. On the contrary, People memorize extremists, as opposed to partisans.

People should speak their mind. Have a view, even if it may piss some group off. When people have a different opinion, they will immediately become more attractive and as an outcome more unforgettable.

TALK AS MUCH AS YOU CAN

People will by no means memorize the person who stands there and speaks nothing. This implies that people have to contribute vigorously to the discussion. Raise questions, demonstrate interest, narrate stories, and share some insight.

BE UNUSUAL

When somebody breaks the social norms, it draws a lot of awareness. There are many approaches to be completely different. The cheapest is to set up funny and appealing answers to typical questions. People will ask questions several times throughout. Consequently, it makes sense to practice great answers.

TRIGGER FEELINGS

In many situations, people will not recall what a person said; others will overlook what other people did. However, individuals shall never forget how other people made them feel.

REPEAT THEIR NAME

When you are introduced to somebody for the first time, make sure you say the name again. It shall prevent you from not recalling the name. For instance, when the other individual says, "Hello, I am Michael," say again, "It's good to meet you, Michael". This not only assist people in remembering their Christian name, but it also makes a positive sentiment. In general, individuals love the sound of their first name and in the situation of a first meeting, using it illustrates that people are serious about knowing the new person.

NARRATE A STORY REGARDING YOUR NAME

Narrative sticks with individuals more than data, so instead of stating a person's name, give the listeners the background on it to make it more motivating.

For instance, give details on the source of the name. This is particularly useful if it is strange and individuals have a hard

177

time saying or spelling it. An additional preference is to clarify how you got the name.

CONVERSATION

If people do not have any excellent stories to narrate, they should try fitting their names into the discussion as much as possible.

People might do this by addressing themselves by name or using their names in the discussion. As a result, the individual will profit from hearing the name several times throughout the discussion instead of just once at the start. It takes a lot of practice to shun sounding proud, but it might be mastered.

BODY LANGUAGE

Unforgettable people are entirely engaged in discussion, both orally and non-verbally. To be occupied non-verbally, people should make sure they have constructive body language. This comprises of an open chest with uncrossed hands, legs facing forward, head and torso up, and shoulders pulled backward.

At the start and end of the discussion, shake hands if possible. During the discussion, keep an eye on the other individual's body language to echo it. If people are lively and using their hands while speaking, the other person should not stand there like a sculpture; they should do the same. In addition, people should Make good eye contact and smile repeatedly.

ASK BETTER QUESTIONS

People will likely be asked the unchanged "how are you?" queries. Assuming the individual is not attempting to respond to these queries exceptionally as recommended; people will go on autopilot and react to them in very customary habits.

Ignite brain movement by engaging the individual with attractive queries. For instance, inquire about what has been the underline of their day. Consequently, it will compel them to reflect and make the speaker look unique from other people.

FOLLOW UP

People should not just collect business cards; they should put them to use instead. They should send messages recapping their discussion. In addition, their email address must comprise their picture to allow people to effortlessly link the name and the face. On the other hand, the picture should be the profile picture on social media platforms as well.

REASONS FOR NOT REMEMBERING NAMES

If people are anxious, fed up, or facing individuals who fright them, they might forget their names. Using an individual's first name is essential to opening doors for people and initiating an early relationship. This could make the individual a new companion for future business engagement.

People should understand the significance of using a different person's name. Occasionally it might assist in perceiving the outcome of using a person's name rather than centering entirely on the anxiety, wary memory, or simple lack of determination to recall a person's name.

Using a different person's name forms a link and is a form of acknowledging them as being extraordinary and esteemed. It makes the meeting consequential for the other individual, and it assists them to feel superior that someone has recognized them. Remembering an individual's first name is considered as being polite and selfless. First impressions matter significantly, and an individual might not get an additional chance to make a concrete and likable impression.

People should be aware that the most ordinary reason for not recalling names is essentially very simple. It is typically because people not keenly listening or not paying sufficient attention. In addition, much of this may stem from anxiety and worry regarding the kind of feeling an individual is making on the other individual. The respond is to offer the person full attention when one is introduced to them and to focus on them entirely. In case someone finds it difficult to recall another person's name, it is because they are worried and so busy distressing about a topic of discussion. Worrying about what to say distracts concentration and memory. Concentrate on the benefits of spending a short but useful time searching about how to make little talk so that you can invite others into your conversations. When introduced to others pay attention so that you may hear their names clearly.

People should ask for the name once more if they do not hear it properly the first time. No one expects people to make a huge deceit of knowing the other individual's name if a person did not essentially hear it when it was said. People must seize the occasion and be definite to say that they did not catch the name, or something related. It clarifies that the name requires to be said once more, perhaps more plainly or gradually. An individual should listen the second time keenly. Occasionally, this is an excellent trick to utilize if somebody was overwhelmed by anxiety, noise, or whatever else has abstracted them. People will frequently be alert that a name has been confirmed and they should use that consciousness to instantly apologize for not listening and requesting the name once more.

In addition, individuals should repeat the person's first name when they are introduced. Repeat the given name unhurriedly rather than rapidly to make it comprehensible. Use the pause in the prologue to also smile and confirm that someone is legitimately satisfied to meet this new individual. Use people's names early on in the discussion, such as at the beginning of the statements or query.

THE ROLE OF COMMUNICATION AND SOCIALIZING IN BUSINESS

Socializing skills refer to the capability of a person to communicate with and recognize their business team. Incorporated with this is the capability to work with others on an individual level and maintain a qualified level of compassion towards them. Understand what other members of the team might be going through, and to purely interact with them on an individual level.

Everybody interacts with is an individual with diverse feelings and desires. That is social skills. Communication ability, on the other hand, entails the ability to make a suggestion or set of orders and express them to the audience in a way that is understandable. These skills shall enable an individual to give plain directions, communicate thoughts to other people, and keep higher management conversant of the position of the entire organization. When social and communicating skills are practice and applied appropriately by a business team, they play a pivotal role in the success of business.

CHAPTER 9: PUBLIC PRESENTATION

Speaking to listeners might be fun and thrilling. But, lack of research or not evidently defining the presentation's objectives and its spectators may make even the best-intended appearance a complete tragedy. Public communication skills are important both in an individual's life and in their occupation. Even if someone does not frequently engage in public talking, increasing skills in this region will increase somebody's confidence and lessen nervousness about situations in which they might be called upon to talk in public.

Even people who live with social nervousness disorder might become self-assured speakers, with proficiency development and management for nervousness.

STRUCTURE THE PRESENTATION

Once the speaker has determined their presentation's purpose and general goal, as well as the listeners, it is time to structure the presentation. The speaker shall need to start this procedure by determining the duration of the appearance.

Take the prearranged time and break it into lesser segments, with each section tackling a detailed task. For instance, the first section should be the presentation opening. In this part, the speaker should offer a synopsis of their presentation or a short précis of the speech, elucidating the subject on why the speaker is covering this subject, and what they hope to achieve.

The subsequently part should tackle the earliest item on the schedule, with the next section tackling the following piece on the agenda. Once the speaker has developed the opening and outlined the next section, they should spend some time pondering about the ending of the appearance. The opening of the presentation and the finale of the staging are the most vital parts and must have the strongest consequence.

ORGANIZE THE ROOM

If possible, the speaker should visit the area in which they will make the public speech in advance. Decide how the audience will seat and decide how the illustration aids that are chosen will appear. Reflect on lighting, room, even the hotness of the room. Think about inserting notebooks and pencils at each chair if members want to take notes. Or, the speaker may desire to have glasses at every seat with a few water jugs if the presentation is going to take long. If the speaker does this, they should make sure they permit time for toilet breaks.

While the speaker does not need to remember the entire presentation, they should make themselves familiar with it through a number of practice runs. Prepare the presentation in full as frequently as the speaker can before giving it to listeners. The more the speaker practice, the more positive they will be and the more confident they will seem to the listeners. If the speaker knows their topic and has sufficiently prepared, they will be able to convey their message. When in suspicion or worried, the speaker should stay focused on their point. Express the thoughts to the topic at hand. The addressees have come to hear the presentation, and the speaker will thrive.

PREPARATION IS VITAL

The speaker wants their speech to run, and that could not occur if they do not take time to arrange for it. That is not a simple goal, however, and it might be done. The speaker should start by setting aside the date and assemble the piece. They should move on by noting down points they want to put across to the audience. Then organize them rationally, so they flow logically from one to the following. After this, the speaker might mix in something more to clutch the audience's concentration.

KNOW THE AUDIENCE

At this point, the speaker knows what to speak about; however, how to put it across to the audience is another narrative. First, the speaker needs to recognize who shall be listening when they speak. To state it differently, the speaker should know their audience. In addition, they should find ways to get familiar with the listeners. Aspire to be friendly with them. Consequently, the speaker must dig up their weirdness, desires, aches, and preference peeves. Be conscious of the age bracket of the listeners. Demographics are an essential aspect of discovering the audience. The speaker does not need a proper survey to get this information. The speaker should interact with the audience in the first few minutes of the speech.

GET SATISFIED WITH THE SURROUNDINGS

The capacity of the location is directly proportional to the speaker's gestures and actions. Big places need huge gestures and extensive movements. Little spaces require the reverse. In a big hall, the speaker needs to plan to have large hand signals and body movements, or else the speaker falls short of engaging the listeners. If the setting is as small as a school classroom, correct consequently. In a tiny space, the speaker rolling their eyes will grasp people's attention. In such a situation, even a half-smile might emphasize a point.

If the speaker checks the speaking site first, they also determine whether they will have the sovereignty to stroll to and fro. Or they will be restricted in a tiny location, like behind a platform. These little details are essentially not tiny at all, and if the speaker thinks systematically about them, they will make all the variation in the speaking engagement.

THE SPEAKER'S APPEARANCE

The speaker must make sure they are groomed and looking good in their favorite attire. When the speaker looks great, they feel great too. On the other hand, if the speaker prefers an informal appear and it is suitable for the event, then they should go for that non-formal appearance. It will make the speaker feel happier and more appealing to equally casual listeners. Audiences at first judge the based on appearance, so the speaker should make an additional effort to dress to command admiration and self-assurance.

PRACTICE

For the time that the speaker is on the stage, their speech depends on how well they practiced. If the speaker messes up, the listeners shall remember him or her for that. That is a sufficient basis to practice and go on practicing. The speaker should record a video of them practicing the speech and revise their strengths and limitations.

When the speaker records their speech, they will also detect whether they speak too slow or too fast. Consequently, they should adjust their talking pace so their audience shall get the most of the presentation. Analysis of the speech on video is as well a way to verify if the speaker has the affinity to talk in monotone. If the speaker does, they should make a point to contrast their tone.

CONFIDENCE develops from picking a topic the speaker likes and studying it well. FRIENDLINESS may be conveyed purely by smiling at the listeners. EAGERNESS and ENERGY shall logically follow when the speaker enjoys the topic and are well equipped. If the speaker feels that their stage presence is missing, they should watch clips of speakers whom they respect.

VOICE CONTROL

The voice of an individual is the most significant tool they will utilize as a public speaker. The speaker should develop the quality of their voice through diaphragmatic inhalation. This is how proficient musicians inhale. It is what assists in making their vocal sound tremendous and allows them to hold notes extensive after most individuals could be out of breath. By doing so, the speaker reduces feelings of breathlessness triggered by speech nervousness.

BODY LANGUAGE

The speaker should consider their body language and the point that it puts across. An individual should Practice standing with a comfortable upright pose. Place the arms at the sides or clinched in front of the speaker, unless they are making a signal to highlight a point. In addition, the speaker should become conscious of their facial expressions as well. This implies that they must match the message they are delivering. If the presenter is giving a cheerful speech, they should try to have a calm and pleasant look on their face.

DELIVERY

When it comes to good public talking, delivery is paramount. Even if the speaker has a good voice and excellent body language, their message shall get lost if the listeners cannot easily follow what the speaker says.

AUDIENCE RELATIONSHIPS

Excellent public speakers are in connection with their listeners. Public talking is more than appearing in front of a crowd and chatting. The speaker should acknowledge the listeners right away and start talking as soon as the audience is settled. This aids to make the presenter appear more like a real speaker and keeps an informal pitch. If the presenter needs to set up the apparatus, they should converse with the audience at the same time to maintain their attention.

On the other hand, the presenter must make eye contact and observe for communication from the listeners. Smiles are an excellent indicator; confused looks might mean that the speaker needs to correct what they are doing. But, if the speaker lives with social nervousness, they should be cautious not to focus too much on downbeat faces. It might be that some people are having an awful day, and the expressions have nothing to do with what the speaker is saying. A fine rule of thumb is to locate a welcoming face at the start of the speech. If that individual appears to be bemused or fed up, that is when the speaker knows it is time to tackle issues with their public talking.

VISUAL AIDS

The speaker should consider the use of visual material. Projectors, video apparatus and computers must be tested out earlier to make sure they are working properly and that the speaker knows how to use them.

The presenter should make sure they do not revise too much information onto any particular illustration. A fine rule to apply is to keep every illustration to six lines. The presenter should make sure any sort of graphics is big enough. This enables the audience to see it plainly. The colors applied should be simple to enable good viewing by the audience.

Outlay should be evidently marked and arrange in order earlier. Flip charts must be arranged in advance as well. When applied during the speech, the speaker should make the print big enough for all members to see. When the speaker is applying these diverse visuals, they should not turn the back to the listeners. The visual aids should be positioned well so the presenter may observe the visuals while looking at the audience.

INFLUENTIAL SPEECH

When selecting a topic for their influential speech, it is vital to reflect on the composition of the audience. Because influential speeches are planned to influence or strengthen an audience's judgment or behaviors, speakers ought to think about what and how the listeners think and believe. The audience may be undecided about the topic, or they might be powerfully opposed, in strong conformity, or somewhere along the continuum. In convincing speeches, it counts where they fall on this scale. For example, if the speaker wants to disagree that abortion must be illegal, and the audience is made up of pro-life activists, the speech may seem like the presenter is preaching to a singing group. But if the audience is made up of stem pro-choice campaigners, the talking would be raising an important opposition to a set of attitude, principles, stance, and actions the listeners was previously committed to.

Influential speakers will not usually speak to listeners that previously fully agree with them or behaving in the manner that the speaker would like. Since those listeners no longer desire to be convinced. But, the speaker may find themselves in states that allow them to plea to a **receptive audience.** These listeners previously know something regarding the topic and are open to the idea the speaker is trying to make. For instance, parents are commonly concerned about keeping their children protected. If the speaker seeks to influence them that they must work with their children to stop them from being taken advantage of on the internet, they are expected to welcome what the speaker has to say. Though they are previously convinced that it is significant to keep their offspring safe, these listeners might not be inclined that they have the need to keep their children safe in an online setting. In order to influence this approachable audience, the speaker should first try to foster **recognition** with them by stressing things they have in common.

CHAPTER 10: COMMUNICATION AND EMOTIONS

Communication proceeds with emotions. Whatever statements we make emit a part of us or affect us in a way or the other. There are situations, however, in which emotions can get stronger and more pronounced. One has to use a more conscious effort to stay on the communication course without being distracted. Emotions, both positive and negative, can influence one's judgment.

While negative emotions make one utter negative statements without due realization, positive emotions can entice one to make commitments that they would rationally have avoided. Thus, one needs to be careful not to exhibit their full-scale weaknesses. The mind reasons by thoughts and body by emotions. When the latter takes precedence, then a communication breakdown inevitably looms.

So how can you take charge of your communications in emotionally charged situations?

EMOTIONAL INTELLIGENCE

It is important at this stage to regard what emotional intelligence means in communications. Success in any technical, social, and business ventures is associated more with the person's emotional intelligence than mental intelligence. An expert who is not able to handle their feelings will lack the virtue of sticking at something to the end. But a novice who shows willingness and commitment to the same activity will soon get it done exceptionally well.

Thus, it is not just what one knows about something, but more importantly, how they handle themselves at it. That gives meaning and value to the whole process and the end result of it. The same is the case with communication. A manager who easily gets angry or frustrated working at something is unlikely to spur success values into the team. Conversely, a mere junior member in a group who exhibits qualities of leadership is more likely to inspire a good influence at that moment.

One is considered to be emotionally intelligent when they can promptly identify what they feel, interpret, and regulate their emotions, understand their impact on others, and manage others' emotions. Pay attention to the following aspects and

note how you will develop at your emotional intelligence and communications.

SELF-AWARENESS

You need to be able to accurately recognize your emotions, strengths, weaknesses, and actions. Further, understand how they affect the people around you. Regardless of what causes you to feel certain emotions, it is important to know how each emotion affects your thoughts and what actions the thoughts lead you into. Evaluate the effective outcome of the would-be actions, and see if it would impact positively or negatively, to what extent and if that is necessary.

Keep track of past events that trigger disruptive emotions in you. Get feedback on how others perceived you under the circumstances and focus on deploying your helpful reactions henceforth. Observe how people respond to your new behavior and adjust accordingly. This positive consideration of feedback can also help you build a team with people who have virtue in the areas of your struggle.

SELF-REGULATION

Beyond being aware of your emotions and impulses, make an initiative to work toward managing them wisely. Consider situations and show or restrain emotions based on what is necessary. For instance, rather than shout at colleagues due to stressful schedules, choose to delegate some of your duties.to reduce your workload. Negative emotions are generally overwhelming. Manage and reduce any negative thought that comes to mind.

Where you are on the wrong, do not blame but take responsibility for your mistakes. It will reduce the feeling of guilt, and others will begin to respect you on that account. However, heated a matter gets, try to respond with calm. You communicate more effectively that way spreading a better feeling to the team. If need calls for it, try to do controlled breathing. Evaluate the situation with objectivity, and in a variety of ways, so you do not get provoked easily.

Mind your vocabulary. Focus on becoming a stronger communicator. Use precise words to describe deficiencies and work to address them. Pinpoint what wrong is going on and fix exactly that. This will help you avoid stewing upon it and magnifying its effects.

Self-regulation will help you adapt to change more evenly, react rationally, and consequently earn respect and trust of others. Too, practice mindfulness, and you will realize your perspective change for the better.

EMPATHY

Work at identifying and understanding other people's emotions. Imagine yourself in another's situation and try to capture the same emotions as they would feel. Learn how to read people's feelings from their verbal and non-verbal cues. Notice how far sheer desperation or excitement can lead people and realize how much it will or must have cost them to come out of it well.

Practice listening without interrupting. Learn to observe and gauge people's feelings. When they have low or negative emotions, do not ignore them. Address them. Take time to understand personalities and surrounding circumstances. For instance, socially anxious people need your empathy first. Learn too, to always keep your body language open with a friendly tonal voice to show your social acceptance for them.

Empathy helps you to respond to concerns genuinely. It ignites compassion and fosters your readiness to help others. It shows you care and helps you deliver feedback. It enhances the bonding and productivity of team-workers. It is not that empathetic statements permit for irresponsible behavior, but rather remind us that everyone has their own issues.

MOTIVATION

Emotional intelligence blends with the right choices in what you do in life. Strive always to enjoy what you do and keep striving towards your goals without too importantly considering money or status. Always remember why you do what you do and have the bigger picture in mind at all times. Know what causes you anxiety and strive to have less of it in life. Set new targets and remain positive and optimistic. When facing difficult moments of challenge or setback, try and find one positive factor about them and work by that. Take time to explain to others why they are valuable, no matter the circumstances. It provides and upholds in them a sense of purpose.

Motivation helps reduce procrastination, foster self-confidence, conquer setbacks, and to keep focused on the goals. Motivation will help you bounce back from adversity into your path of success. You will ask positive questions about challenges and draw from them lessons that will strengthen your muscles of hope and positivity, spreading it to the team within an instant.

SOCIAL SKILLS

If you turn out to be emotionally intelligent, then you will first manifest it by effectively managing your relationships with the view to realize mutual benefits. Work at developing your communication skills and listening to feedback with an even mind. Provide praise where necessary, and provide constructive feedback at all times. Strive to be a team player regardless of status or regard.

Listen to others and show empathy. Aim to create and maintain personal relationships with individuals rather than just groups. When conflicts arise, resolve them through accumulating the parties' views and lobbying for compromise, where necessary, for the good of everyone.

Social skills are necessary for you to build rapport with people as well as earn their respect and loyalty. In circumstances where the best decision is the unpopular, social skills help you earn people's trust nonetheless. Interaction and identity with individuals can inform how their abilities can be blended for better productivity. Being a sociable person makes others feel comfortable sharing their ideas and concerns with you.

COMPOSURE

Composure describes the total personality that you present yourself to be in the face of adversity or crisis. It is your signature of reaffirmation that says despite how clumsy things may seem midway, the very outcome of your endeavors is already established and it does not depend on the moment to moment confusions that may arise. Composure is when a clearer picture of tomorrow is cast in the dull circumstances of the current moment to make certain the way through.

It is important for leaders to see adversity from a lens of opportunity too. What presents in the course of another needs to be worked out or worked at. It could be a necessary factor by itself or pointer to another, and it must not be feared or ignored. Crises result where composure misses. When people sense signs of leadership naivety and unpreparedness, they feel unsafe and insecure and withdraw their trust from the leadership. Hence leaders must be composed in order to show poise and control if they shall lead the team through tough times.

GET EMOTIONS OUT OF THE WAY

Train yourself to go beyond emotions when you want to solve problems of any sort. Think about what you have to do and dwell on that, and the emotions will subside. Do not be dramatic. Do not yell at colleagues or get overly animated gesturing at them. Control your emotions and let your body language respond in a similar manner. This will help you to remain objective through the resolution process.

Have a strong will and use that to keep yourself composed as you handle issues at hand. You are needed to show concern and care in such a manner that reassures that all hope for the goals is not lost under the prevailing situations.

DO NOT GO PERSONAL

Things do not always play out logically. The company-politics, for instance, and many other dynamics can influence the factors around the ongoing processes and pose challenges. It's a collective responsibility, and everybody is involved. So, you do not need to try justifying your thoughts and actions of how this could have been avoided. Focus on staying committed to solving the problem and returning systems back to normalcy. That is all that is needed for you.

Take control and show that you are doing it well so that you have the support of everyone. Do not get every issue too close to the heart. Do not allow external noise and politics to rule over your thinking and decision-making capability.

BE OPTIMISTIC

Keep a positive attitude. You can afford a narrative that gives inspiration and hope. Have the resolve to get things together and better, and stay reminded of your leadership expertise, experience, and role. Show strength, smile, and show your sense of compassion.

Set the right pace and tone. Positive-mindedness gets to work by itself to begin neutralizing chaos, so you follow on to set the right course of correction and advancement. As you do this, focus on harnessing everyone's positive values and setting the correct momentum for everyone's good.

BE BOLD

Act beyond fear. Be assertive but not controlling on the team. Project confidence and cool and calm personality. Remind yourself and everyone that it is not the crisis that hurts but the outcome that will benefit. So be ready and do not show fear in the face of it.

It is impossible to act rationally under the attack of fear. Courage expands your mind and keeps you focused on the way and how you want to come out of it strongly. Rather than expecting the worst to happen, analyze the current situation, and get in action to manage and resolve it at the earliest opportunity.

RESPOND DECISIVELY

Do not show doubt. You do not need to know the answer right away to do this. Decide how you want to come out. Know that you have the required means and abilities. Challenges do not come to stop course but to spur commitment and determination. It is not the relative easiness you expect but the resolve to set things right and that's what must be done at all other expenses.

Speak with conviction, exude your confidence, and show authority. When everyone knows the way, they quickly shift their focus that way. And the sooner they know it and do that, the better for all.

TAKE ACCOUNTABILITY

Decide and stand up to your responsibility to undertake every required step to solve the problem before it goes out of hand. The decision to do this in itself begins to defuse the problem and brings the very environment where it sprung to a pause.

This takes the recognition that until you take your rightful place and initiate action, no one will.

DO NOT ACT NEW

Approach the issues with a sense of elegance and grace. Problems come to refine something in you, and that is something you will willingly pay attention to throughout the course. Show patience with people and for the execution process, exercise your active listening skills, and employ a compassionate approach that will ease anyone's hardship during the moment.

CHAPTER 11: BODY LANGUAGE AND NON-VERBAL CUES

Body language in all its forms is critical in any communication process. They not only initiate and sustain communication;

they also significantly influence its meaning, and can sometimes be the entire message than what one would have to say. Depending on how well one uses their body language, they stand a greater chance of benefitting compared to those who do not know how to use it at all.

The first impression, mostly, is not the result of speech or conversation, but the bodily presentation and the kinds of messages that the cues communicate concerning us. How one dress, poses, and gestures for salutation, their tonal voice, their facial expression, how they occupy and utilize space, etc. speaks volumes about their personality. Indeed, it emphasizes or contradicts the verbal messages depending on the degree of congruence achieved during communication.

Looks are a vital part of body language that invokes people's interest in us and draws them closer for further interactions. You can invest in time and effort to create a comfortable, open, and inviting atmosphere that will facilitate increased social interaction for you. Learn how to use an open body language to engage others and put on the appropriate appearance that will make you look and feel more sociable to others.

SMILE OFTEN

A warm smile will invite anyone to want to converse with you. It puts them at ease and implies of you as having a great time. If you want to make, friends smile. It makes you appear friendly, pleasant, and open to having a conversation. A genuine smile engages the whole face and makes your eyes glow, and your face looks brighter.

A fake smile, on the other hand, can be noticed and interpreted against you. So, goes for a half-smile. Giving smiles makes you receive smiles as you gain access to people's hearts and lives. Smiles do not only invite for conversation; they also retain people's interest in you. It creates a whole host of sociable people around you, and that's what good life asks and offers.

A smile is said to help reduce anxiety, blood pressure, and heart rate. These help you to be relaxed during social interactions.

PROJECT AN OPEN POSTURE

A person who feels rather uncomfortable around people naturally closes off in their posture. If you are mindful enough to want to connect with people, then become more mindful of your posture. Do not literally shut people out of your social space without knowing it. Are you feeling nervous or in a bad mood? That is not for people to know. Stand upright, arms at sides and lean toward the person speaking to you.

Practicing to open up in your posture in the rightful gatherings even when you do not feel like it naturally helps improve your mood and draw people toward you. Always be reminded of this. Angle yourself toward people when they are speaking so they know you are interested in their words. Listen actively and show your involvement in the conversation.

Face the speaker right with your face, body, legs, and feet. Keep your arms open and unfolded. Pay attention to the posture you present to others because they pay attention to it before they decide to draw nigh or away.

MAKE EYE CONTACT

Conversations begin at good eye contact – at least with strangers and acquaintances. Eye contact stimulates good emotions in the other person and creates silent energy that creates the connection. Sufficient eye contact is enough to keep your colleague conversing with you.

Too short eye contacts speak of you as being shifty-eyed and could be a sign of insecurity. Longer than usual eye contact is characteristic of one telling lies. Do not keep looking down at your feet or the floor. It makes you appear shy, which can be unfortunate for you.

Look up and be aware of the surroundings, notice people, and they will pay attention and want to converse with you. Smile to people while they approach you and maintain regular eye contact throughout your conversations. Eye contact makes you appear trustworthy and interested in the topic of conversation.

BE STILL

Do not fidget. It is unlikely that the very people are the reason for your nervousness, boredom or unhappiness. And even if they are, feeling low harms you not them. If you are approachable, you must project positive emotions. Biting your hand nails and twirling your hair portray you as being bored or nervous and sets you aloof.

Beware. Take a few deep breaths when you feel the urge to fidget. Avoid touching your face frequently, tapping your foot, itching yourself, etc. Be still and flexible and comfortable. Show attention and focus on what is going on. Do not be too still to seem like a zombie or suspicious of yourself. Note how you adjust your sitting or standing posture and how you nod and let your stillness show your composed, relaxed self and mood.

MIRROR YOUR COUNTERPART

Beyond showing interest in the message that the other person is saying to you, develop an interest in their body language too. Mirror them during a conversation without making them uncomfortable. Observe their gestures, their posture, and stance and try to reflect that back to them. Mirroring does not mean imitation. You do not need to do it to a level of perfection.

Effective mirroring helps to build trust and connection. A company in which employees enjoy a positive rapport with their leadership benefits from employee loyalty. It is, however, not advisable to try to mirror someone who is senior or superior to you. They may find it impolite and forceful.

MIND YOUR WARDROBE

Buy yourself clothes that make you appear friendly and inviting. They will make you appear presentable as well as boost your self-esteem. If it doesn't naturally occur for you to make appropriate choices of cloths, consider getting assistance from friends or vendors or stylists. They will help with well-suited options and appropriate for your body type.

Flattery clothing that is well-tailored and versatile will portray you as composed, self-assured, and pleasant to be around. Take good care of your clothing and observe hygiene with them. They should be clean and pressed crease-free.

DRESS FOR THE EVENT

Be modest in your dressing. It portrays your sense of judgment and poise. Dressing appropriately shows that you are respectful and happy to be at the event. Be sure it is not only acceptable but also inoffensive. You want to receive positive attention, not negative. If you are not sure what dress code to use, consider getting in touch with the host for clarification.

Mind your hairstyle too. Ask your hairstylist for what works for your hair texture and face shape. A fitting hairdo helps you get noticed as collected and outgoing.

MIND YOUR COLORS

The colors of your garments influence how people perceive and react to you. Colors of calm fall in the ranges of blue, green, and warm earth tones. They make you appear more confident, reliable, and approachable. Shades of red present a more assertive, not very approachable or friendly personality and may naturally make people stay away from you.

Be careful what colors you choose for interviews. Navy and green tend to set people at peace more promptly. Be sensitive to how you accessorize to your dressing. You want to accentuate your better looks, but not distort your friendly tones. So be mindful of what colors you put in your wardrobe and use them to project a personality positive and welcoming.

USE A NAME TAG

If you are at work or a taking part in hosting a business or corporate conference, then you will find it rewarding putting on a name tag. Many employees do not like using the name tag because they lack loyalty or total commitment to their jobs. But it relays a different kind of message for the positive-minded who know what their businesses mean to them, and what they want out of it.

The name tag shows you as being willing, open, and available for conversation and networking. This way, people are drawn to you for conversation, creating more chances for business partnerships. You can have a few giveaways that will warm up your potential customers or partners and make them anticipate the same experience collaborating with your business.

AVOID DISTRACTIONS

When a conversation is stuck, give it your full attention. Be mindfully present. Let your counterpart know it. Practice your active listening skills. Listen for as long as is required without interrupting and allow the speaker to finish their thought. Listening plays a significant role in establishing quality relationships with others. Beyond appearing to be friendly and approachable, it is also the first sign conversationally of being a patient caring person.

Make eye contact, smile, and nod slowly to show that you are listening and are consciously focusing on them. The more you are noticed to be an active listener, the more you are approachable by many for conversation. Be polite, appear composed and at ease and without hurry. Do not keep checking at your watch or phone. Do not get side-tracked into surrounding conversations around you at the expense of your speaker's or listener's attention.

VALIDATE THE OTHER'S FEELINGS

As much as possible, do not be disapproving of the personalities. Show empathy and respond when appropriate in a fitting manner when one is narrating a situation of sadness. Do not question their emotional impulses right away. Do not offer advice in not asked. Such times are ones in which one seeks your emotional presence and support rather than guidance.

Empathy is a virtue by which many will find you to be supportive, understanding, and comfortable to be around. And it will not take them long to observe this in you and desire your association.

ASK QUESTIONS

Asking questions is one of the prompt ways to tell people that you are interested in hearing more of their story and are keen on the details. When you do not understand a point, or you want to hear more of their perspective on a specific topic, ask for clarification and elaboration. Demonstrate your attentiveness to what is being said. Make the conversation more interesting by gesturing appropriately and responding with positive comments.

If you think you have a common interest with someone, throw them a question on that ground. They will be happy to pick up the conversation with you quickly. Be a good conversationalist and consciously call your whole conversation assets to action with the view to enjoy the moment and create a lasting bond with your new-found friends.

Be sensitive and quick to notice and give a memorable first impression. It takes a moment for one to decide to approach you. It, therefore, requires you to be fast to give that smile, make eye contact, and warm up to your new friend.

Dressing in shades of blue relays messages of a more approachable individuality in you. Consider them for your coded messages of calmness, dependability, and sociability. Avoid aggressive statements in every form, at least until you have struck a deal with your new friend. This mostly happens on the second or subsequent meetings.

Be sensitive to age differences in your interaction with people. Mind yours too. While the older prefer formal dressing, the younger prefer casual. Consider your vocabulary with the elderly and differentiate from the younger. While the body language may not vary so much, but it is important to align it appropriately in this regard.

Learn to speak more quietly than loudly. Where there is a connection, parties like to put in a little effort to contain their conversation between themselves. It is also a natural way of telling the rest of the world to allow you time first to finish. Be calm. It communicates power over flaws. Calmness emanates from mental, emotional, and physical convergence in strive and purpose. Who doesn't want to associate with that virtue?

Finally, you can't change your face, but you can change your look. Take care of your skin. It speaks volumes about your health inside. Do not be artificial. Authentic relationships are founded between authentic personalities. And the benefits are amazing. Love yourself too, and your values of personality will effortlessly find a way into the hearts of other people. It pays to want to be of social essence with people and the world around you.

CHAPTER 12: CULTURAL DIFFERENCES AND COMMUNICATION

WHAT CULTURE HAS

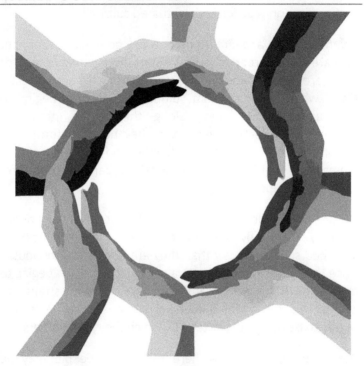

Cultures are not just many. They are also diverse. A person in their daily life comes across many instances in which he invokes his sense of judgment by minding and balancing between factors; social, economic, environmental, etc. Working styles vary from place to place. Age, nationality, gender, race, ethnicity, and even sexual orientation can each be considered to be a culture, but they will vary in respect to the prevailing circumstances.

People do not set out to create cultures. Cultures are a natural derivative of social interactions. That is, cultures are created through communication. Traditional literature is passed on to generations through communication. The characteristics of culture include roles, rules, laws, customs, and rituals. These aspects become imparted in how people communicate hence shaping their communication practice. And the resultant communication practice is perpetuated culturally.

Communication and culture do not only go hand in hand, but they are also interdependent. We start picking up our cultures at just around the same time we start learning to communicate. Also, when people from different cultures begin to communicate, they bring along their prior interaction behaviors. But as they get along, they begin to form their custom culture how they identify and co-exist among themselves. That is why, for instance, company cultures differ and relationships are unique.

Culture may be defined primarily as the set of values that are uniquely shared by a group of people. These values are absorbed subconsciously than they are imparted consciously. Once they begin developing in a person, the person begins to recognize what is normal and right versus what is strange or wrong. This, resultantly influences how one thinks, acts, and keenly to be noted, the criteria by which they judge others.

We importantly mention here that while people may be identified and described by their cultures, it is unjustifiable to define and judge them exclusively on that ground. Family upbringing, individual experiences, and aspirations, education, and information can influence a person's outlook and consideration of people and situations. All in all, the diversity that cultures present: at the core of it is the very natural desire to associate and cooperate with others and leave a positive mark.

HIGH-CONTEXT VERSUS LOW-CONTEXT

Cultures can be considered to be high-context or low-context. High-context cultures encode and cast their communications into the context while low-context extracts their communications from the context. As such, high-context messages are more implied or indirect, while low-context messages are more express or direct.

In many corporate seminars today, the medium of communication is normally influenced by these contexts. It is not absolutely the degree of industrialization but the contexts that determine how people effectively communicate. This requires the speakers to be aware of the audience and try to communicate as much as possible in an appropriate manner.

In high-context cultures, personal bonds and agreements, though informal are considered more binding than formal contracts. They operate on trust. The intention of any meeting is not necessarily for corporate reasons but personal bonding for a lasting connection and mutual interaction. Conversely, low-context communications prefer legal documentation in meticulous wording for any contracts or agreement to be considered valid. It does not matter the face behind a deal, as long as it is efficacious.

High-context communications leave more unspecified messages. The listener has to draw understanding from the context. The context includes cues and in-between-line hints. They generally find it disrespectful and disturbing to use certain words, or associate with certain values and thus avoid exclusive use of words in communication. The low-context cultures code their messages in an explicit and specific manner.

High-context cultures leave the meanings of their messages in what is not said. The listener needs to interpret the body language, silences, and pauses, or relationships and empathy, etc. For instance, when one wants something from you, you need to go your way to evaluate the details and provide for them even when not expressly mentioned. You do that because you mind your relationship with them and are watching out for their welfare and success. The low-context messages are accurate and precise with detail, including timelines. It is about what is required not about what one means to the other.

TIME IS SEQUENTIAL OR SYNCHRONIC

Cultures that consider time sequentially see it as a linear commodity that is to be spent, saved, or wasted. The past does not matter any longer as it is gone. The present must be optimally utilized to make the most out of it. Time saved is time created. Time wasted is irrecoverable, and a loss is incurred. The synchronic types consider time as always available and seize every moment to capture the full experience of it; however, much it takes.

The sequential types give exclusive attention to one thing at every moment until it is completed and then progress to the next. Focus for concentration, optimize for efficiency, and produce with promptness because that is how tasks will be completed faster and the next ones initiated upon in their time. Time is money — the synchronic type work to have everything at the same time. To them, the past, the present, and the future are interdependent. So, if you plan anything, it must be the long term, not the short term.

You take the phone call, while serving the client right before you and at the same time admiring the child playing with the toys in the waiting area. That is being synchronic. Perceived in this manner, it can be quite troubling how, for instance, they turn up for meetings. The sequential type considers lateness as a result of one who plans poorly and is disrespectful. The synchronic type finds the concept of timeliness as being childish impatience.

The sequential thoughts know that you can use personal effort today to influence the future. But since there are many dynamics that affect the distant future, you take particular interest in the next quarter results. If you feel results are at par with your expectations for the period, then you are way on. The same principle works in relationships. Their existence depends on what you have done in someone's favor lately. The synchronic types consider the past to be the context in which to understand the present and prepare for the future. Relationships to them are the most important and durable thing, and the bonds established run back and forth in time. It is preferred to favor friends and relatives in dealings of business.

THE AFFECTIVE VERSUS THE NEUTRAL

The affective are the kind of personalities that readily show their emotions. If it does not add up, it is condemned, and the feeling of it must come out in a pronounced manner possible. If something is good and exciting, then the affective will smile broadly and compliment using the best terms possible. The affective will grimace, smile and laugh or shout, cry, and walk out, and that offers them a solution for the situation. The neutral opt for the neutral approach to matters. It is not that the neutral does not feel, but they strive to keep their emotions controlled and subdued throughout their dealings.

The neutral is mindful of how much emotional display they make. They do not find it adequate to get excited or underwhelmed unduly. They focus on the task at hand and try to avoid personal distractions midway. The affective, on the other hand, prefer expressing their feelings openly. They get personal so fast and stop to engage rationally on the issue at hand. While the neutrals can get empathetic when their counterpart is upset, the affectionate once agitated care less. They relieve their emotions and leave you to soothe yourself.

The neutral believe every idea can work. It only needs to be so tested and if approved, adopted for full implementation. The affectionate are opposites in this regard. They want facts and numbers at hand to decide on whether an idea can work or not. They try not to get involved deeper than they think they should. They draw boundary lines and go only that far.

However, you classify your culture, you will find that the differences are not necessarily just that, but a second thought at it will reveal how they are consistent with each other. For instance, the fact that the synchronic strives to live and experience the moments to the fullest does not mean that they are not mindful of the future. At the same time, the sequential do not disregard the past. They learn from past mistakes and draw facts from past observations, for instance.

Generally speaking, no one lives exclusively by a certain culture's rules and totally disregards the others'. Is it possible the neutrals lose their patience after some time waiting? How about the affectionate sometimes managing their emotions in certain moments? The high-context cultures seem to share properties with the synchronic and neutral cultures and are more common among eastern continents. The low-context, the sequential and the affective, common in the western world, seem to supplement each other quite significantly. This understanding of the dynamics at the macro-level can first inform how you respond to people at first meeting and subsequently.

CULTURES AS COMMUNICATION BARRIERS

Cultures shape mindsets, languages, signs, and symbols. The criteria for rating people and their values vary between cultures. Hence what one finds important might not mean much to someone else from a different culture. Different cultures with different languages encode and decode their messages differently and hence, may obstruct communication.

Within the same languages, words may have different meanings depending on contexts, and that can lead to misunderstandings. Also, signs and symbols, including body language and gestures, can be quite different and with varied meanings across cultures.

Stereotyping can be a major negative consequence of cultural differences. When preconceptions about people guide your interactions with them, then you are bound to provoke negative feelings that bar communication. Behaviors, beliefs, and religions when not well controlled by members can cause misconceptions by sending wrong messages. When one is unsure how to behave in the presence of a stranger from a different culture, then they may become highly anxious. This anxiety might prevent them from initiating or responding to a conversation when prompted.

CROSS-CULTURAL COMMUNICATION

It refers to how people from different cultures communicate. It is helpful to try to exchange and mediate between cultural differences through the use of language, gestures, and body language. Try to listen more, or get an interpreter where possible so that you hear the exact real meaning of what is said other than the words in their plain meaning. Consider learning the elementary grammar of foreign languages and gestures of the cultures you interact mostly with.

Also, learn to become cognizant of your perception towards other people and make every effort to avoid prejudices and to stereotype. Accept differences and be open to learning from others. You cannot know everything. However, you communicate to people of other cultures, seek feedback, and open up to channels of communication. Take charge of your emotions. Do not get in the habit of surprising others for not being considerate with your expressions of feelings.

When responding to people from a different culture, do so with the view to provide the right response rather than the right message. Part of understanding their culture should be to consider how they take turns during a conversation. There surely cannot be one best suiting approach to communication between people. The success of it can only perhaps be in understanding and respecting the differences. It boosts creativity, teaches new perspectives, teaches new ideas, and contributes to world unity.

CONCLUSION

The book offers you an exciting discussion on the way communication has serious implications on life and existence in general. Through what the book covers, you have learned how you can use communication to make life better and survive. The aim is for everyone to be able to survive through embodying various survival abilities. This book shows you that communication is one such important survival ability that one has to strive to be competent at.

The book offered deep insights into how communication should be executed in various situations and circumstances. This is in light of the fact that communication is the means by which people make their thoughts and feelings known to others. It is a primary avenue of interaction and hence this book makes you realize that a limited life could be reflecting limited communication abilities.

Though this book, you can unlock various opportunities in your social life. This is through the discussion on communication as a tool of making friends, initiating interactions and sustenance of relationships. it can unlock opportunities for jobs and self-growth as well as has been discussed about nailing the interviews.

As social beings, this book exposes you to the way we can exercise our nature through communication. This is through guiding elements of being funny and the cultural bearing on communication. It offers some deep psychological explanations of how communication is processed in light of the various circumstances in which it happens.

Dear Reader

I am an emerging writer and, with the sales made from the book, I can continue my studies to publish other books on the subject. I would appreciate an honest review from you.

Thanks for your support

CPSIA information can be obtained
at www.ICGtesting.com
Printed in the USA
BVHW040539100221
599717BV00008B/968